Twayne's English Authors Series

Sylvia E. Bowman, *Editor*

INDIANA UNIVERSITY

Colin Wilson

TEAS 181

Colin Wilson

Colin Wilson

JOHN A. WEIGEL

Miami University

TWAYNE PUBLISHERS

A DIVISION OF G. K. HALL & CO., BOSTON

Library of Congress Cataloging in Publication Data

Weigel, John A.
Colin Wilson.

(Twayne's English authors series ; TEAS 181)
Bibliography: p. 145 - 51.
Includes index.
1. Wilson, Colin, 1931- — Criticism and interpretation.
PR6073.I44Z9 828'.9'1409 74-28137
ISBN 0-8057-1575-4

MANUFACTURED IN THE UNITED STATES OF AMERICA

For my students: David, Jane, Marilyn, Michael,
Richard, and Susan — and all the others who have
kept faith with the Outsider.

Contents

About the Author

John A. Weigel is Professor of English at Miami University, Oxford, Ohio. With advanced degrees in literature (Western Reserve University) and psychology (Columbia University), he has both alternated and crossed fields. As a Ford Foundation Fellow in 1952 and 1953 he pioneered research in verbal behavior and information theory as a much-needed antidote to the then fashionable psychoanalysis of literature and literary figures. Thus he is personally familiar with Colin Wilson's Outsider-syndrome insofar as his behavioral approach to literature was once anathema to most humanists.

Dr. Weigel authored the first book-length study of the British novelist, Lawrence Durrell (Twayne's English Authors Series; paperback edition by Dutton, 1966). He has published numerous professional articles as well as satiric verses, and reviews scores of novels annually and lectures on timely topics. At present he is completing a critical biography of the American psychologist, B. F. Skinner, and researching a study of the American novelist, John Barth.

Preface

Soon after the publication in 1956 of his first book, *The Outsider*, twenty-four-year-old Colin Wilson was invited to lecture at Cambridge University. No more ingenuous victim has ever been called up for a stoning, and no more incorrigible hero has ever so valiantly survived. For a week after the visit, so the story goes, all Cambridge debated the proposition: Colin Wilson — bloody fool or great writer? There was no formal decision; but the debate, although on a reduced scale, still continues. Time and Wilson's industriousness — the "bloody fool" has produced almost two books a year since then — have cooled the hot need to polarize; and today hostile critics of his ideas have learned to respect Colin Wilson as a man.

In short, the controversy over Wilson's value has become an honest and open one, indicating the viability of the issues. Furthermore, recent changes in the philosophical climate have redefined Wilson's significance as a thinker who has persistently challenged pessimism and despair. Determinism and the hard-core existentialism of such philosophers as Jean-Paul Sartre are going out of fashion. Sartre had cautioned against optimism as bad faith; cheerful humans had been warned against hope; and they had been told that beautiful experiences were fraudulent insofar as they made things seem better than they are.

Colin Wilson's brand of existentialism, the explication of which is the main burden of this study, has dared once again to exalt freedom. Men are invited to reject despair as the human condition, and they are urged to depose Absurdity by breaking it up into little absurdities that can be defined and attacked. In this context, the philosophical essays, the novels, the biographies, and the critical writings of Colin Wilson have become more and more meaningful.

This study of Colin Wilson contends that the man and his works have often been seriously misapprehended, resulting in distorted judgments of Wilson's significance. When any one of the many items which compose the impressive whole of Wilson's canon is considered in a narrow context, certain qualities, such as the good faith and the derring-do of Wilson's total work, are obscured. For example, using a jeweler's scale to weigh great chunks of rock is as inappropriate as measuring any one of Wilson's novels on an exquisitely wrought *literary* scale. Wilson is not a stylist; therefore, his most significant effects are seldom achieved with delicate nuances or with pastel epiphanies. Since any genre he uses is quite frankly exploited for its idea-conveying potential, his novels and his fable-like fantasies, which for Wilson are devices for promoting his deepest commitments, have often been discounted for the wrong reasons as well as occasionally praised for equally wrong ones.

As Wilson has matured as a thinker, his style has, however, improved. He has always been concerned about his effectiveness as a writer, but his objective is not to find the irreducible form of an idea, for he is a persuader rather than a poet. Perforce, there may always remain a gap between his urgency and his message. He has, however, tried to shorten that gap at times by taking rhetorical risks at the cost of logic by resorting to paradoxes and parables when exposition and argument fail. Indeed, many a great teacher when confronted with a difficult question has answered: "Let me tell you a story." Similarly, Colin Wilson utilizes rather than serves literature.

Because there have been few analyses of Wilson's work, this study contains much explication that could have been omitted in a work about a more familiar writer. The attempt here has been to honor the needs of all those who want to know about Colin Wilson and his books in order to understand his message. But some compromise was required since a critical study cannot proceed both longitudinally and vertically — both along a time line and via categories — without awkward redundancies. The decision has been, therefore, to divide Wilson's significance into several categories — such as phenomenon, philosopher, novelist, and critic-of-all-trades — and to acknowledge the possible use of this book as a reference guide to one or more of Wilson's many concerns. The Chronology which precedes the text provides a minimum framework for the whole, but of course neither such an outline nor the brief biography in the first chapter can do complete justice to the complexities of a life as productive as Colin Wilson's.

Finally, in order to clarify Wilson's message for nonspecialists, technical terms have sometimes been defined in a relatively unsophisticated way. Philosophers and psychologists would do well, of course, also to consult Wilson's texts. In all fairness, any ignoble errors here are my fault. All the noble errors, such as heroic heresies, however, may be attributed to Wilson himself, who is accustomed to carrying such burdens valiantly.

Special thanks go to my research assistant, Bob Webb; to my student-friends who typed: Tom McClellan, Becky Rofsky, Jill Frederick, Jerold Simms, and Marilyn Maloney; and to Kathy Keho, secretary extraordinary.

JOHN A. WEIGEL

Miami University
Oxford, Ohio

Acknowledgements

Permission to quote brief passages has been graciously granted by Colin Wilson and the following publishers:

Arkham House, Sauk City, Wisconsin *(The Mind Parasites).*
Arrow Books, London *(Sex and the Intelligent Teenager).*
Atheneum Publishers, New York *(Bernard Shaw: A Reassessment).*
Calder and Boyars, London *(Strindberg).*
City Lights Books, San Francisco *(Poetry and Mysticism).*
Crown Publishers, New York *(Chords and Discords, Lingard, Voyage to a Beginning, The Philosopher's Stone, The Schoolgirl Murder Case).*
Farrar, Straus & Giroux, New York *(Rasputin and the Fall of the Romanovs).*
Victor Gollancz, London *(Religion and the Rebel).*
Houghton Mifflin, Boston *(Beyond the Outsider, Introduction to the New Existentialism, The Outsider, Ritual in the Dark, The Stature of Man, The Strength to Dream, The Violent World of Hugh Greene).*
Putnam's — Coward, McCann & Geoghegan, New York *(Encyclopedia of Murder, Origins of the Sexual Impulse).*
Random House, New York *(The Glass Cage, The Occult).*
Taplinger, New York *(New Pathways in Psychology).*

Chronology

1931 Colin Wilson born June 26 in Leicester, England, to working-class parents.

1940 Begins writing at the age of nine. Discovers science fiction and ransacks public library for books on psychology, philosophy, and related areas.

1942 Identifies himself as a genius. Begins period of depression but continues to write and read. Discovers George Bernard Shaw.

1944 Writes first work, a summary of all knowledge (not published).

1945 By the age of fifteen, knows who he is and where he is going. Feels "as big and as important as the universe."

1947 Begins to keep the journal which is eventually "filtered off" into *The Outsider*. Graduates from the Gateway Technical School.

1948 Terminates position as an assistant in the Gateway School. First short story published in a Durham factory magazine.

1949 After trying odd jobs accepts posting to Rugby as civil servant. Called up for national service in Royal Air Force in September.

1950 Receives medical discharge from Royal Air Force followed by odd jobs and a trip abroad. Spends short time with Raymond Duncan, wealthy patron of young writers, but finds himself an unsuitable disciple.

1951 Returns to Leicester and more odd jobs. Marries Dorothy Betty Troop; goes to London to find a home for his family.

1953 Wilson and first wife separate. Speaks in Hyde Park as member of London Anarchist Group. Has "disquieting" experiences such as sex episodes and "vastations." Goes to France in fall but soon returns to England. Meets Joy Stewart, who eventually becomes his second wife.

1954 Writing in British Museum while sleeping on Hampstead Heath. More odd jobs.

1955 Works on *The Outsider*, which pours out of him "like molten lava."

1956 John Osborne's *Look Back in Anger* produced at the Royal Court Theatre on May 8, and the "Angry Young Men" are launched. On Saturday, May 24, *London News* reviews *The Outsider* (to be published May 26) and announces: "A MAJOR WRITER — AND HE'S 24." Both book and Wilson become sensation.

1957 *Religion and the Rebel* published. Critical massacre begins. Wilson's publisher advises him to abandon writing and find a job. Unshaken in his determination to become the world's greatest writer, Wilson moves to a cottage in Cornwall; also visits Germany.

1958 *Declaration*, a volume of essays by the "Angry Young Men" (minus Kingsley Amis), appears. Wilson's contribution identifies him as guerrilla philosopher, religious wing.

1959 *The Age of Defeat* (published in United States as *Stature of Man)* receives mixed reviews, but the Outsider cycle is under way. Buys a house in Gorran Haven, Cornwall.

1960 First novel, *Ritual in the Dark*, received with less hostility than expected.

1961 Ten-week lecture tour of United States results in Wilson's liking both lecturing and the country. Second novel, *Adrift in Soho; Encyclopedia of Murder* (with Pat Pitman).

1962 *The Strength to Dream* published.

1963 A productive year: *Origins of the Sexual Impulse; The World of Violence (The Violent World of Hugh Greene* in United States); and *Man Without a Shadow (The Sex Diary of Gerard Sorme* in United States).

1964 The production line continues: *Brandy of the Damned (Chords and Discords* in United States); *Necessary Doubt*, a novel; and *Rasputin and the Fall of the Romanovs*, a biography, published.

1965 Two more publications this year: *Beyond the Outsider*, the sixth volume in the Outsider cycle; *Eagle and Earwig*, a collection of critical essays.

1966 Writer-in-residence at Hollins College in Virginia. *Sex and the Intelligent Teenager; The Glass Cage*, a novel; and *Introduction to the New Existentialism.*

1967 Visiting professor at the University of Washington in Seattle. *The Mind Parasites* published. Expanded version of *Brandy of the Damned* published as *Colin Wilson on Music*.

1969 *The Philosopher's Stone*, another science-fiction fantasy; *Voyage to a Beginning*, an "intellectual autobiography"; *Bernard Shaw: A Reassessment*.

1970 *The Killer, Lingard, Poetry and Mysticism, The God of the Labyrinth (The Hedonists)*; the drama, *Strindberg*; and *The Strange Genius of David Lindsay* (with J. B. Pick and E. H. Visiak) published.

1971 *The Black Room, A Casebook of Murder; The Occult* indicates a definitive turn of Wilson's thought toward the psychic.

1972 *Orders of Assassins; New Pathways in Psychology*. Wilson has now clearly defined his position.

1974 *The Schoolgirl Murder Case*, first of a projected series of twelve "mysteries." Other plans and proposals are extensions of Wilson's previous research and commitments. Approaching his middle forties, Wilson can survey and add up an achievement equal to men twice his age. Evaluations and reassessments are in order as his many books and articles can no longer be taken lightly.

CHAPTER 1

The Outsider as Phenomenon

COLIN Wilson's first book, *The Outsider,* appeared in 1956 with a bang. Almost instantly an international best-seller, it quickly became one of the most controversial items in recent literary history. As a matter of simple fact, this earnest product of a personal agon, although designated by its young author as the most important book of its generation, was not meant to be sold in every market place. Addressed to a passionate few, something untoward happened when it was taken up by a less passionate many. Colin Wilson as well as the product was put on trial; and even the critics who had at first enthusiastically endorsed *The Outsider* — some without having really read it — revised their opinions. Because they were embarrassed at having overestimated the work, they implied that Wilson had tricked them with malice aforethought. Time, however, has darkened such rancor; today, even Colin Wilson's most severe detractors praise his energy and his enthusiasm. Yet more often than not the Colin Wilson phenomenon is still improperly measured, and now is the time to set the record straight.

Colin Wilson was a prodigy, and he suffered the consequences; for prodigiousness both attracts and repels. Either extreme of the bell-shaped curve which describes the distribution of human ability is awesome. Most people are normal, they like being normal, and the tendency in genetic events to produce more normals than abnormals makes prodigies disturbing. A prodigy defies the regression phenomenon by which, in the long run, everything tends toward the mean: bright parents generally have children less bright; tall parents, children less tall; and such averaging is reassuring. In contrast, prodigies are rare. Young geniuses have to fight hard for adult success; normals have ways of cutting superiors down to palatable size. Inevitably, enthusiasm for Wilson's erudition gave way to skepticism which redefined his scholarship as namedropping. Wilson's wisdom was proportionately downgraded, and it has taken many years for the backlash effects of Wilson's prodigiousness to subside. Less emotional judgments are now in order.

I Voyage to a Beginning

When Colin Wilson was thirty years old, Sidney Campion wrote a book about him which only partly pleased the maturing boy-wonder. "Why should anybody be interested," he asked, "in the biographical facts about any man under the age of eighty?"[1] Thus it is not surprising that Wilson found it necessary to justify publishing his autobiography at an age that did not meet by half his own minimum of eighty. "My intention in these pages," he says of his *Voyage to a Beginning* (1969), "is to lay bare, as honestly as I can, the basic aims and motives of my work and to relate them, where it is relevant, to events in my own life."[2] The tone of this work is significant in that it indicates that Colin Wilson has not lost his nerve. His high confidence in himself, which is sometimes misunderstood as arrogance or conceit but which is essential to his program, is intact. Colin Wilson feels now that he is just beginning and that " . . . twenty years of work have not taken me far. (This is not modesty. I know that I have come further than any of my contemporaries. I would be a fool if I didn't know it, and a coward if I was afraid to say so.) But at least the years seem to have taken me to a point from which I can make a beginning" *(Voyage,* 336).

II Early Years

Colin Wilson was born June 26, 1931, in Leicester, England. Leicester, the county seat of Leicestershire, is noted for making boots and shoes; and it is neither a charming nor an exciting city. Aware at an early age of the "vegetable mediocrity" (*Voyage,* 40) of his working-class background, Wilson *chose* greatness, feeling rightfully that his choice was limited to that or nothing; and he wasted little time in getting started in his pursuit of it. Leicester could offer him basic schooling; books; and, perhaps most important of all, movies. Wilson has testified to the impact of the cinema upon those who are born with "the burden of dullness" not shared by middle-class and upper-class children. Movies provide therapeutic romances for underprivileged youths, and he was grateful for the quick and easy brush with enchantment that he found in the new "talkies."

In Wilson's search for heroic models, the young man glorified those scientists whose courage led to the pursuit of facts. Such facts,

Wilson knew, could be used as weapons against the ordinariness of home and school. Only science, Wilson believed at the time, could save him by leading him to Truth; and he was determined to make no compromises. Certain that fortune was on his side, yet too bright not to appreciate the strength of "an overwhelming, monstrous triviality, a parasitic triviality that ate its way into all values" (*Voyage*, 33), Wilson was forced into the kind of urgency that makes or breaks. He knew that he was destined for highest significance — but not without a fight. "Throughout my childhood," he remarks in *Voyage to a Beginning*, "I was always aware of the two opposing impulses: distrust of the world, and the sense of immunity, complete confidence" (25).

Noting more and more that he was different from others around him, Wilson without quibbling identified that difference as his genius. "The first glimmering came about the age of twelve," he told Sidney Campion; "and I was fully and unashamedly aware of my genius at fifteen, and from then onwards I went ahead with knowledge and self-assurance which carried me through thousands of difficulties. I knew who I was, what I was, and whither I was going. . . . I felt as big and as important as the universe."[3]

The son of working-class parents born into Leicester-mediocrities had to feel big in order to survive. For those who prefer genius tempered with modesty, Wilson has recently emended his youthful self-evaluation in *Voyage to a Beginning:* "Looking back on it all, I can see that I was not half the prodigy I thought I was. The kind of knowledge I picked up could have been acquired by an industrious eleven-year old without an atom of real scientific ability. But it was just as well that nothing disillusioned me. I got used to thinking of myself as a prodigy; it became a mental habit that inoculated me against the prevailing 'fallacy of insignificance' " (34). In any event, he appeared prodigious enough for his schoolmates to call him "Professor" — and Colin did not deny that claim to superiority. In fact, he wrote an essay about it, fearing meanwhile that God might strike him dead for doing so. Later, after reading through *Practical Knowledge for All*, a six-volume encyclopedia he bought at a church bazaar, the boy proceeded to write his own history of everything, turning out "articles" on physics, astronomy, chemistry, geology, and aeronautics. Later he added essays on philosophy and mathematics. By Christmas of 1945, the fourteen-year-old Wilson had completed six volumes of his synopticon; but he wisely realized that his summary of all knowledge was still inadequate. His decision to discontinue the work in progress was a postponement, however, rather than an abandonment.

At an early age Wilson had turned a spare room at home into a laboratory. Although he wrote an essay defending Albert Einstein, he began to lose part of his interest in science after the atom bomb was discovered, for he had intended to make that discovery himself. No project seemed too formidable for him to contemplate; but the quasi-madness in his method was then, as it still is, part of the essence of his method; and, not surprisingly, he was subject at an early age to alternating periods of depression and elation. These valleys and mountains of existence became his measuring periods, and they predicted the moods he later identifies as "vastations" and "peak experiences."[4]

The young man concluded his formal schooling at the age of sixteen. During some erratic and half-hearted attempts to arrange for a higher education, he spent a dismal year as an assistant in the Gateway Secondary School, the technical school from which he had graduated and where he "learned a disproportionately small amount" *(Voyage,* 40). After that experience, Wilson supervised his own education. As an autodidact, he was a relentless taskmaster, for he was determined to excel despite his poverty. He says in *Voyage to a Beginning* that his decision not to become "some kind of combination of Schopenhauer, Ronald Firbank, and H. P. Lovecraft" was forced upon him because he simply could not afford a "tower" (47).

Wilson identifies the period in 1947 after he left school as the most crucial one of his life. During a long series of menial jobs, he reaffirmed his commitment. Thinking of himself as a philosopher and a writer while performing insignificant tasks for pay he focused his conflict: "The 'two worlds' now seemed to stand facing each other, and open war had been declared: on the one hand, the futile world of 'everyday life,' on the other, the possibility of a way of life that should be completely *meaningful,* creative, and self-conscious" *(Voyage,* 48). Reading and writing took up all his spare time. He read Shaw until he knew most of his work by heart. He wrote plays and short stories and began to keep a journal into which he poured his frustrations and from which eventually came the passages and allusions which are crammed into *The Outsider.*

In 1949, Wilson passed a civil-service examination and was entitled to white-collar security as a clerk in a tax collector's office, which he soon found less tolerable than manual labor. Rather to his relief, he was called in September by National Service; but his brief career in the Royal Air Force was, to put it mildly, undistinguished. His account in his autobiography of how and why he was finally discharged in 1950 emphasizes his belief that a man should control those aspects of his fate which he can, even though his larger destiny may swing with factors beyond his ken. By distorting the truth and implying he was homosexual, Wilson succeeded in obtaining a discharge. Six months after entering service he "came out, having been certified 'nervously unstable' and altogether unsuitable" (73).

Optimism, which formerly had been suppressed, now dominated Wilson's thought; he began to plan. His first step was to accept his own diagnosis of what ails mankind as valid rather than as merely a function of his youth and timidity. Unabashedly sure that he himself was relatively well, Wilson accused mankind of being so sick that it did not even know it was sick. For Wilson, man was so firmly in the clutches of an octopus-kind of killer that only here and there did someone break free: "Occasionally the sickness lifts, the stupidity rolls back; for hours or minutes the senses seem to stretch antennae out into nature; the mind is aware of new, subtle implications in every thought; man achieves something of the confident mastery of a god. Then the octopus regains strength; the tentacles wind round the heart and brain; the state of emergency is back; again the fight against suffocation" (*Voyage*, 75).

Believing that some men conscientiously resist that octopus but are then penalized by their blinkered, sick fellows, Wilson perceived a pattern in the resistance and in the counterresistance. He divided men into a minority of courageous resisters and a majority of conforming nonresisters. The latter brand the minority "outsiders" because they do not understand them. This insight began to obsess the young man. Inevitably he identified himself as one of the minority destined to solve the problem of how such outsiders might survive in a culture dominated by nonoutsiders. The plight of these mavericks seemed to him so critical that he capitalized the name of the category. The eighteen-year-old Outsider certainly felt he had hold of an important idea, but he had more living to do first before attempting to promote it fully.

III Young Adulthood

Sometime in his late teens Wilson discovered sex. His autobiography refers to his relationships with two wives and several mistresses and specifies some bedroom action that is more amusing than shocking, for the details were solemnly added at the request of the publisher. The prurient, however, will be disappointed; for, although Wilson is always frank, he is not a sexual athlete, and sometimes he is delightfully ingenuous. Referring to his liaison with a girl called Sylvia, Wilson says in *Voyage to a Beginning:* "I then made the pleasant discovery that I did not have to choose between philosophy and sex; I could have both" (274).

In 1950 Wilson tried working as a laborer and as an actor. He also sampled the alleged joys of hitchhiking and learned that for the most part they are overrated. Nevertheless, he was in good spirits that summer. Everywhere he went he carried with him Friedrich Nietzsche's *Zarathustra* or Walt Whitman's poems, and read Lao-tse's *Tao Te Ching* while working as a ticket seller in a fair. In the fall of 1950, he went to France, spent a short and unproductive time in Raymond Duncan's "Akademia," and then visited a friend in Strasbourg before returning to Leicester in December. Sidney Campion quotes from Wilson's diary for the period which shows how dedicated he was at the time. "I would be God," Wilson had written. "Human beings seem very unreal to me. I know now what drove Vaslav [Nijinsky] 'mad.' It was the remembrance of what is possible. . . . To seek for God and to find sexual complications, a wife, a Diaghileff, would drive all geniuses to frenzy."[5] After reading the works of William Blake (whom he discovered through Joyce Cary's *The Horse's Mouth*), Wilson decided not to settle for anything less than becoming another Shakespeare. About this time he also perceived that both madmen and murderers are artists, and he decided that to achieve greatness one must suffer almost unto death. Being still young and untried, however, he was not able to avoid contretemps.

In June, 1951, he married unwisely but honorably a woman ten years his senior. The day after the registry-office marriage, the young groom went to London to find work in order to support his new responsibilities. A son, Roderick Gerard, was born to the couple; and Wilson enjoyed for a while domestic security. He also kept to an incredibly full reading schedule: "I seemed to have stumbled upon a large number of important books that no one else knew about: Nijinsky's *Diary*, Wells's *Mind at the End of Its Tether*, Granville-Barker's *Secret Life*, Hesse's *Steppenwolf*." He had also just discovered *The Gospel of Sri Ramakrishna*. "I decided," Wilson guilelessly notes, "that I must one day write a book relating them all" (*Voyage*, 123).

And he indeed did try to relate them all — not in just one book but in a production-line series of philosophical, critical, and fictional works, producing almost two books a year after 1956 as well as writing numerous articles. By the autumn of 1952, however, Wilson had not yet hit his stride. His meal-ticket jobs were becoming increasingly depressing, and his marriage was disintegrating. He candidly confesses in his autobiography that ". . . I saw that this marriage was an irrelevant interlude, a long diversion from my purpose: it would *have* to end" (31). By January, 1953, Wilson and his first wife separated; and he took a job in London as a porter in a hospital, a place which "reeked of sex" and which provided "the perfect atmosphere for incubating some future Jack the Ripper" *(Voyage*, 135). This experience was later used in the final version of his first novel, *Ritual in the Dark*, which he was working on intermittently during these years, along with *The Outsider.*[6]

By 1953, Wilson was surer than ever that he was to be among the great ones. He accepted his marital disaster philosophically: "If a relationship could not be established on my own basis, I was prepared to forego the relationship. I classified myself with Nietzsche, Van Gogh, T. E. Lawrence, Nijinsky, as a mystic and as an outsider, as someone driven by an evolutionary urge that transcends normal personal motivations" *(Voyage*, 134). That year, identifying with Shaw, he joined an anarchist group and made several speeches in Hyde Park. He also acquired some important friends, among them Bill Hopkins and Stuart Holroyd, whose literary careers paralleled and reinforced Wilson's for a time.[7] Late in the year, he decided to leave London and return to Paris, where his dream of freedom in expatriation turned into a nightmare. After vainly trying to make a living by selling subscriptions to the *Paris Review*, Wilson gave up and returned to Leicester, "hoping vaguely," he remembers "that fate might have changed its policy toward me" *(Voyage*, 159). Apparently it did, for shortly thereafter, while working in a Leicester department store, he met Joy Stewart, who was to become his second wife and whose importance in his later life he has always emphasized.

After Christmas, 1953, Wilson returned to London; and he recalls in *Voyage to a Beginning* that 1954 as a bad year: "I was beginning to feel like Raskolnikov just before the murder in *Crime and Punishment* when he suddenly has the feeling 'he would not go on living like that.' I was sick of putting up with fools, working at jobs I hated, never having the leisure to work continuously at *Ritual*" (188). So Wilson bought a sleeping bag and began sleeping on Hampstead

Heath, which was not far from the British Museum, where he spent most of his days reading and writing. He was bemused when Bill Hopkins, who was something of an opportunist, praised him for thus building up "the Wilson legend" by emphasizing his austerity and dedication. Although Wilson himself never really liked sleeping outdoors and being poor, after the success of his first book he realized that becoming a legend is not without profit. His nights sleeping on Hampstead Heath made him seem a new Thoreau; his days studying in the British Museum Reading Room made him seem a new Voltaire. Actually, although the night air may not have affected his health, reading in the British Museum proved to be lucky, for there he met Angus Wilson, then a museum official. Angus Wilson was friendly, offered to read Colin's manuscript, the one which became *Ritual in the Dark*, and his endorsement did Colin Wilson no harm.

Colin interrupted his heath-sleeping that summer for two short holidays, one to the Lake District and one to Cornwall. In Cornwall, he and Joy camped near the cottage where he and his family later settled. There he had time to contemplate and plan his future. "I was becoming increasingly aware," he comments later, "that human beings die inside a prison cell of themselves, unless they can find salvation by directing the whole being outward, toward something impersonal" *(Voyage*, 195). That fall he concentrated on writing and reading in a rented room in Brockley; he typed a new version of his novel, and studied the works of St. John of the Cross, Jan van Ruysbroeck, Giovanni Scupoli, William Law, Jakob Böhme, and Walter Hilton — mystics who he hoped would help him advance his program. He yielded to the fact that "he was becoming more and more obsessed by the question of what one could *do* in a civilization like ours, that has no real symbol of spiritual values" *(Voyage*, 196). Motivated and increasingly informed, he began to write the book that became *The Outsider*.

In January, 1955, Wilson took a night job at a coffee house in the Haymarket, one of the few jobs he has ever really liked. This one was ideal, for he found the manageress and his co-workers friendly, and he was free to spend his days working on *The Outsider*. "It was pouring out of me," he says, "like molten lava out of a volcano, and I knew it was good. I was writing of myself, seeing myself mirrored in Van Gogh, Nijinsky, Nietzsche, T. E. Lawrence. I was writing of men who had been half-forgotten — Granville Barker, Leonid Andreyev, Hermann Hesse." Wilson was confident of the value of his work. "This book will be the *Waste Land* of the fifties, and should be the most important book of its generation" *(Voyage*, 200).

Wilson sent the outline of *The Outsider* to Victor Gollancz, for he had judged correctly from his inspection of a religious anthology published by Gollancz that this publisher was likely to be sympathetic with the subject. Gollancz agreed to publish the work,[8] and the period just before the publication of *The Outsider* was a pleasant time for Wilson. He had a few kind and interesting friends, and he could afford to wait patiently for what he hoped would be a thoughtful albeit quiet reception of his first book. But, by the end of 1956, Colin Wilson had fully sampled the equivocal flavor of success.

IV *"A Major Writer at Twenty-four"*

Literary history records two significant events in May, 1956: the opening of the John Osborne play *Look Back in Anger* at the Royal Court on May 8, and the publication of Colin Wilson's *The Outsider* on May 27. The so-called "Angry Young Men," who all began almost immediately to disown the label, were beginning to direct their youthful anger against mediocrity and complacency. On Saturday, May 24, the *London Evening News* headlined its review of *The Outsider:* "A MAJOR WRITER — AND HE'S ONLY TWENTY-FOUR" *(Voyage,* 210). Other rave notices followed from such diverse critics as Edith Sitwell and Philip Toynbee; and, in America, *Time* called the work "a compelling intellectual thriller."[9] Wilson, whose name was soon public property, responded at first with pleasure mixed with awe: "The phone rang steadily for a week. The following day — Monday — an immense pile of letters arrived for me; it seemed that every friend I had ever had decided to write and congratulate me. The *Sunday Times* rang and asked if I would like to do regular reviewing for them at forty pounds a review. I gasped at the sum. The BBC and television rang and asked when I would be available to make recordings. . . . Reporters were arriving at a rate of four a day" *(Voyage,* 210).

Wilson's account of his instant success, from the perspective of more than a dozen years later, is steady and honest. When he refers to the cult aspect of the Angry-Young-Men syndrome applied to him, Osborne, Amis, John Wain, and several others who happened to be young and producing at the same time, Wilson says: "I wasn't in the least angry — except about my years of struggle; and now that I was recognized, even this hardly applied" *(Voyage,* 210). Yet he cooperated and allowed himself, for example, to be photographed in his sleeping bag for publicity releases. The lad from Leicester was used to indifference and to mediocrity, but he knew little of hostility and nothing of professional jealousy. Although he was puzzled by that hostility and jealousy, he was charmed by the fame and fortune. For the first time in his life he could afford to eat well and to buy all the recordings he coveted. He not only went to many parties but also threw a monumental one himself. Along with Iris Murdoch, Angus Wilson, and John Osborne, such notables as Stephen Spender and Sir Herbert Read dropped in. According to Campion, Wilson at one point during the party modestly announced that the celebration was also in honor of Angus Wilson's recent novel, *Anglo-Saxon Attitudes*. There was, however, one tense moment when Mary Ure pointed out that Osborne's play *Look Back in Anger* was authentic, whereas Colin Wilson's book was simply made up of quotations. But, in general, it was a successful evening for the prodigy from Leicester.[10] In the following weeks, Wilson tried to adjust to his fame, but he made a few predictable mistakes. For example, flattered by many offers to give lectures, the new celebrity began by accepting them all, "traveling in quick succession to Oxford, Cambridge, Eton, Northampton, Leicester, and even Glasgow" *(Voyage,* 211).

Wilson's British publisher, Gollancz, promoted the book, for he knew it was a potential best-seller. In September, 1956, Houghton Mifflin published *The Outsider* in the United States, where, despite some negative critical reviews in fastidious journals, the popular media enthusiastically endorsed young Colin Wilson as a genius.[11] What followed, however, Wilson calls "a grotesque parody of success" *(Voyage,* 216). Although he had, in his youthful and reckless enthusiasm originally appointed himself the "heir of Eliot and Joyce" and identified himself unabashedly with Nietzsche, Nijinsky, and Shaw, he had never foreseen "being treated like a film star, an intellectual prodigy, a boy wonder" *(Voyage,* 211). Wilson asked himself: "What had all this to do with *The Outsider?* The book was about Nietzsche's vision on a hill called Leutsch, and the vastation experience of William James, and Nijinsky's 'God is fire in the head,' and Van Gogh's 'Misery will never end, and Ivan Karamazov's 'It's not God I reject; I just want to give Him back the entrance ticket' " *(Voyage,* 216).

The public reaction to *The Outsider* soon began: "Six months after its publication," Wilson dispassionately notes, "it was the general opinion among English intellectuals that *The Outsider* had been a craze that had died a natural death, and that I should now be returned to the obscurity from which I had accidentally emerged." He knew what was happening, if not why: "I got the feeling that every journalist in England wanted to throw his stone on the cairn that covered my dead reputation. The Americans also joined in the fun. No country is more eager to hail celebrity; none more delighted to see its downfall" *(Voyage,* 219). Wilson himself now attributes most of the dramatic reversal of opinion concerning *The Outsider* to hostility toward his quick success and, understandably enough, not to any inferior quality of the book itself. Kenneth Allsop, who analyzes the story of 'the angry decades,' refers to a "mixture of honesty and naiveté in Wilson" as largely responsible for the emergence of hostility. Allsop tells how Wilson at a literary luncheon "airily referred to *The Outsider* as 'a fraud, dished up to look like an impersonal appraisal of our time when really it expressed a completely personal vision.'" The news report of that speech was headlined: "WILSON ADMITS HE IS A FRAUD!"[12]

Depressed but not defeated by the backlash, Wilson decided in 1957 to leave London. His move to rural seclusion, however, was motivated by an event which had little to do with his book. He and Joy were living together in his flat in Notting Hill. One day Joy's father, in a dramatic scene misrepresented and exploited by the press, threatened Wilson with a horsewhip. Soon thereafter Wilson took a cottage in Cornwall, where he began in comparative seclusion to solve the "success problem" by getting back to work.

V *The Massacre*

What Sidney Campion calls "the real massacre" of Colin Wilson began after the publication of his second book, *Religion and the Rebel,* on October 21, 1957.[13] Philip Toynbee, who had originally extravagantly praised *The Outsider* by comparing Wilson with Sartre, was evidently anxious to redeem his "*faux pas.*" He called *Religion and the Rebel* "a rubbish bin" *(Voyage,* 240) and Perry Miller wrote: "To call these essays sophomoric is to dignify them. . . ."[14] The American press joined in the manhunt.[15] Wilson's response to the attack was all the more valiant for its possible rationalization: "There was a kind of consolation in all this. My reputation had quite clearly touched rock bottom. It could go no lower. This did not necessarily mean that it now had to rise; but at least it could not fall" *(Voyage,* 240 - 41).

When Wilson's publisher, Gollancz, advised him to stop writing for a year or two — to take "a regular job" — Wilson refused to consider such a dismal retreat, despite the fact that his play, *The Death of God,* had been rejected by the Royal Court Theatre that same year.[16] As a diversion, Wilson accepted an offer to lecture in Oslo to a university audience; and there he discovered that he enjoyed lecturing. The students were interested in ideas, and he found the entire scene compatible with his concept of what he was trying to do. "Here, being a writer," he discovered, "seemed to involve all the things I used to dream it involved before I published a book; a sense of intellectual vitality, of participating in literary history" *(Voyage,* 242 - 43).

Wilson was not the only one of the "Angry Young Men" to be severely treated by critics; for, fairly or unfairly, his friends Bill Hopkins and Stuart Holroyd were virtually destroyed about the same time. The public was being warned against these young prophet-types — these "Messiahs of the milkbars." Colin was called "the existentialist's Billy Graham."[17] Kenneth Allsop describes the "crime of the Wilsonians," whom he classifies as neo-Nietzscheans: "This peasant army (all the group, I think, grew up in provincial industrial towns) have had the temerity to clump into the academic closes where the trainee priests are learning their catechism from A. J. Ayer and Bertrand Russell, and break in with a loud errand boy's whistle. 'Throw your logical positivism out of the window and stick up your hands,' they shouted. They have irritated and offended the orthodoxy."[18]

VI *Productive Years*

In 1958, Wilson worked all the harder at offending orthodoxy by completing his third philosophical book, *The Age of Defeat* (published in the United States as *The Stature of Man)* in a few weeks. It was originally intended as Wilson's contribution to a work on "the vanishing hero" to be written jointly by Bill Hopkins, Stuart Holroyd, and Wilson; but, when Gollancz offered to publish Wilson's essay separately and sent along an advance of five hundred pounds, Wilson and his friends agreed to separate publication of Wilson's contribution. *The Age of Defeat* was published in 1959, an event which Wilson confesses he did not look forward to. "It had been two years since *Religion and the Rebel* had been hatcheted to death," he says, "and in that time I had managed to avoid publicity. But there had been no noticeable change in the tone of press cuttings. My name still got mentioned if someone needed a symbol of intellectual pretentiousness, or unfounded generalization, or an example of how hysteria can make a reputation overnight" *(Voyage,* 257).

The reviews of the third book, however, were generally polite if dismissive. The *Times* reviewer, Wilson notes, "remarked that I was obviously 'here to stay.' " To which Wilson answered without hesitation: " 'He's damned right I am' " *(Voyage*, 257 - 58). Finally his first novel, *Ritual in the Dark*, appeared in 1960; it was received fairly well and sold significantly; but Wilson's claims for his solemn novel were not always credited. From 1960 on, Colin Wilson accepted the responsibility of his role as husband and father along with the more equivocal obligations of his role as professional writer. The sharp hostility of the backlash was subsiding, but he continued to experiment with writing dramas while working on a series of sequels to *The Outsider* and a series of correlative novels. In 1960, his play, *The Metal Flower Blossom*, was more or less stillborn in a production at Southend-on-Sea, with Wilson playing a minor role. In 1961, his second novel, *Adrift in Soho*, based partly on the material in the unsuccessful play, was published. Although not badly received, the event was blurred by some unfortunate publicity in which Wilson agreed to simulate a televised quarrel with another writer. Often Wilson's problems with his public image have to do with his youthfulness and his apparent insouciance.

Encyclopedia of Murder, which Wilson coauthored with Pat Pitman, appeared in November, 1961. And that same year Wilson undertook a ten-week lecture tour of the United States, which he enjoyed. He responded to America as a vital place, one which he empathized with as his "natural home" *(Voyage*, 303). In 1962, appeared *The Strength to Dream*, the third volume in the Outsider cycle. After this volume Wilson's work began to be apprehended as an *oeuvre;* and, although he did not always receive serious attention, the *fact* of Colin Wilson was accepted. In 1963, he published his third and fourth novels, *The World of Violence* (called *The Violent World of Hugh Greene* in the United States), *Man Without a Shadow (The Sex Diary of Gerard Sorme* in the United States), and a fourth volume in the Outsider cycle, *Origins of the Sexual Impulse*.

In 1964, he published a series of essays on music, *Brandy of the Damned (Chords and Discords* in the United States); another novel, *Necessary Doubt*; and a biography, *Rasputin and the Fall of the Romanovs*. In 1965, he published the sixth volume in the Outsider cycle, *Beyond the Outsider*, and also *Eagle and Earwig*, a collection of reviews and critical essays (most of which had been printed earlier in periodicals). A summary of his philosophical position, *Introduction to the New Existentialism*, appeared in 1966 together with another novel, *The Glass Cage*. *The Mind Parasites*, the first of two novels in the fantasy-tradition of H. P. Lovecraft, appeared in 1967, and *The Philosopher's Stone* in 1969. *Voyage to a Beginning*, an extended version of an autobiography which had been privately printed serveral years before, and *Bernard Shaw: A Reassessment*, also appeared in 1969.

Wilson's appraisal of his status in 1969 underlined his almost obsessive ambition: "If this body and brain of mine could be driven on for another hundred years or so, I could probably solve all the problems of philosophy single-handed. As it is, I have been thinking pretty consistently and continuously since the age of twelve, and it will take me another twenty years to create a basic terminology, to complete the foundations of a real philosophy" (*Voyage*, 336).

As part of his full-speed-ahead to the "real philosophy," Wilson began after 1969 to refine his philosophical commitments and his literary techniques. Two novels published in 1970, *The Killer* and *The God of the Labyrinth*, enlist mystery, murder, and detection in the good cause. The significance of the poetic experience to Wilson and its relationship to his increasing interest in occultism resulted in a book-length critical study called *Poetry and Mysticism*. An unconventional drama, *Strindberg*, and another critical study, *The Strange Genius of David Lindsay* (coauthored), filled out the list for 1970.

The next year Wilson added a third item to his projections-into-the-future novels, *The Black Room*, which is a carefully worked out parable exhorting preceptive men to potentiate consciousness before they perish. Also appearing in 1971 were two more projections of Wilson's enthusiasms: *A Casebook of Murder*, which explores killing and punishment as perversions of man's creative instincts, and *The Occult*, an ambitious study of paraphenomena and superconsciousness. In 1972, Wilson rounded out his personal psychophilosophy with two more studies: *Order of Assassins* explores the psychology of murder, and *New Pathways in Psychology* is a definitive statement of Wilson's commitment to humanistic, optimistic psychology such as that taught by his friend, the late Abraham Maslow.

By 1974 Wilson's rate of publishing slowed down somewhat, but his work schedule did not. In that year he published *The Schoolgirl Murder Case*, the first of a planned series of twelve "mysteries" suitable for adaptation to television. He still continues to research the facts about occultism, an increasingly pertinent topic, he believes, in today's confused ethos. He also continues to explore the various dimensions of crime, working on a series of articles for a proposed "crime encyclopedia."

All in all, the time is a propitious one for Wilson's interests. Many young people have discovered the inadequacies of the facile enthusiasms of the preceding generations and are willing to study the subjects which concern them: supernatural phenomena, the role of sexuality, the rationale for crime, and speculations about the future relevant to science fiction. More than one admirer of Colin Wilson has recently revived the legend that Wilson is the most important writer alive. Back in 1956, of course, there was no doubt about it — either in Wilson's opinion or in that of the careless critics who turned *The Outsider* into a sensational success without having read it very carefully. This time, however, Wilson's success is not a flash, for he has finally earned the honor of being taken seriously by those readers he meant to take him seriously.

CHAPTER 2

The Outsider as Philosopher: I

THE nature of man is still moot. Free will vies with determinism to fix the responsibility for what man does and why he does it. Although some philosophers have hoped to reconcile determinism and free will by classifying man as *both* phenomenon and thing-in-itself, certain problems remain. In the first category, man's behavior remains as completely determined as all phenomena; in the second category, his behavior is undetermined and thus he remains morally responsible for his decisions. The traditional conflict between placing blame on, and assigning credit to, outside forces and inside decisions is still much debated. A man's "will" is usually credited with his faults but not with his virtues *by others*, but he himself is likely to reverse such a judgment by taking personal credit for his virtues but blaming outside forces for his faults.

A fair but necessarily complicated approach to Colin Wilson is to evaluate him as a free agent who willed his own career and as a phenomenon of the times. As the latter, his emergence as a controversial philosopher was predictable; *his* part in the event was minimal. As the former, however, he is to be credited with the courage to rebel against deterministic philosophies and to insist that man is free to improve himself and his community *if he wants to*. In one sense, Colin Wilson is both heroic and inevitable. As a freedom-espousing philosopher, he chose for himself a big job, namely, to diagnose and to cure mankind's sickness.

I The Outsider

The Outsider (1956), the first and still most famous of Colin Wilson's works, contains most of his virtues as well as most of his faults.[1] While most writers use courteous formulas to help the reader, the young Wilson scorns rhetorical devices; and he also copies burning passages from his journals directly into his work-in-progress — sometimes inaccurately but seldom without crediting his sources. Convinced of the importance of his insights, he piles generalization upon generalization. Sometimes, however, he simply says what he feels and lightly dismisses a serious problem with an ingenuous comment such as "It looks like an unanswerable question, and we had better pass over it for the moment" (219).

Wilson knew the British school tie and accent were not accessible to him, and so his "style" never aspires to elegance. Withal, however, *The Outsider* is a compelling work — a refreshingly enthusiastic synopticon of an earnest youth's eclectic and extensive reading. Wanting to know everything as soon as possible, the young researcher often yields to interesting-looking detours; and such digressions are less pretentious than his main-line concerns and are often quite charming. In general, Wilson's method in his first work is unsophisticated. A host of characters from literature, life, and history are made to bear witness to support a thesis which is constantly being altered as the result of the accumulating testimony.[2]

The first witness Wilson calls upon is the lonely hero of Henri Barbusse's novel, *L'Enfer*. Dubbed "the anonymous Man Outside" (11), he is a poor creature who spends most of his time peering through a hole in the wall of his cell-like room at the life of people next door. Obviously frustrated and lonely, "He is an Outsider," Wilson explains, "because he stands for Truth" (13). The second witness is H. G. Wells. Citing Wells's *Mind at the End of Its Tether*, a testament to dying in which the writer proposes that the world is running down, Wilson earnestly begins his defense of the Outsider's sensibility: "His case, in fact, is that he is the one man who knows he is sick in a civilization that does not know it is sick" (20).

The next witness is Sartre's Roquentin, the journalist-narrator in *Nausea*. Like Barbusse's hero, Roquentin "alone is aware of the truth" (26). As Wilson conscientiously distinguishes among Barbusse's, Wells's, and Sartre's approaches, he sees Barbusse as an empiricist, Wells as a rationalist, and Sartre as a combination of the two. Among other Outsiders, Albert Camus' Meursault in *The Stranger* reminds Wilson of Ernest Hemingway's Krebs in "Soldier's Home," who as a war veteran is alienated from self and family, and also of Harley Granville-Barker's Evan Stroude in *Secret Life*, who is too honest to believe in God and too sensitive not to be miserable about his honesty. Fast on the heels of this improbable group, Wilson summons witnesses from Hermann Hesse's *Demian*, *Siddhartha*,

Steppenwolf, Narcissus and Goldmund, and *The Glass-Bead Game.* Classifying Hesse's seekers after truth as "Romantic Outsiders," Wilson concludes: "Considered as a whole, Hesse's achievement can hardly be matched in modern literature; it is the continually rising trajectory of an idea, the fundamental religious idea of how to 'live more abundantly' " (66). Warming to his subject, Wilson credits Henry James with three Outsiders: Roderick Hudson *(Portrait of a Lady),* Lambert Strether *(The Ambassadors),* and Milly Theale *(Wings of the Dove).*

Because literary projections are often distorted by the aesthetic context, Wilson turns next to witnesses who have *lived.* As examples of "real" Outsiders, Wilson calls upon T. E. Lawrence, Van Gogh, and Nijinsky. Although all three were defeated, each had found an inner source of power: for Lawrence it was his intellect, for Van Gogh his artistic sense, and for Nijinsky his body, and each "concentrated on a discipline that would make the source accessible" (102).

At this point Wilson recognizes clearly that he must deal with transcendents: "It is a question no longer of philosophy, but of religion" (106). The Outsider, because he is more sensitive than others, has special needs. He differs from others in that his "pain threshold," a term Wilson takes from the American pioneer psychologist, William James, is lower.[3] Thus Wilson's next witnesses testify to increased susceptibility to pain, which in turn leads to increased awareness, which in turn leads to intensified pessimism as the evidence accumulates that man does not *really* live by his alleged beliefs. The Outsider *must* believe in the relevance of his insights and his sensibilities; yet those very insights and sensibilities tell him that his insights and sensibilities are probably irrelevant. "It is this *irrelevancy* of a man's beliefs to the fate that can overtake him," Wilson points out, "that supplies the most primitive ground for Existentialism" (112). Such apparent irrelevance can finally be tolerated only by referring it to a bigger plan.

For example, no priest can comfort one who relies only on evidence; for evidence must always be supplemented by faith. The Outsider is motivated to use his faith to help him gather evidence that most apparent irrelevance is *really* relevant, and this obsession with relevance and irrelevance is the mark of a true Outsider. To such a person, the case for increased awareness rests on the advantages to be derived from feeling more and more. Because the Outsider has lower thresholds, he is capable of ecstasy and despair. Unfortunately, however, because of his special awareness, he is incapable of the ordinary evasions that help the mass of men survive the quietly desperate day. As a result, the Outsider is likely to have trouble with mundane details such as making a living and protecting his health. When he wearies of so much tension and wants to change, to be more like others, he becomes sad; for he feels that, in wanting to be more nearly ordinary, he is betraying himself.

Withal, however, that kind of despair is not the essence of the Outsider. The Outsider, Wilson insists, "does not prefer *not to* believe; he doesn't like feeling that futility gets the last word in the universe; his human nature would like to find something it can answer to with complete assent. But his honesty prevents his accepting a solution that he cannot reason about" (120). One temporary solution is Romanticism. Classifying Nietzsche as a Romantic, Wilson insists that Nietzsche was searching for salvation although his hopes for a new religion were frustrated. The philosopher was misunderstood even by those who called themselves Nietzscheans. Wilson's undisguised empathy with Nietzsche resembles the excitement many youths feel when they first discover Colin Wilson.[4] Nietzsche wanted to alert the world, and so does Colin Wilson. "Intellect is not enough . . . Zarathustra made it clear in which direction the answer lay: It is towards the artist-psychologist, the intuitional thinker" (146). More and more, as Wilson corrects and refines his position, he emphasizes intuition as a reasonable faculty: he *thinks* his way to the importance of *nonthinking*. He must praise the noncognitive or intuitive functions precisely because they have "thoughtfully" defined the cognitive or reasoning functions as limited. Thus Nietzsche interests Wilson because the older philosopher helps him escape the trap which his acceptance of the traditional thinking-feeling dualism has sprung on him.

His next witnesses, associated with the Nietzschean superjob of confounding intuition and intellect, are Count Leo Tolstoy and Fëdor Dostoevski. Tolstoy "resembles Nietzsche and Kierkegaard in that he reached religious conclusions while finding it impossible to support the orthodox Church — another feature common to Outsiders" (149). Dostoevski's life, however, personally bears witness to the ability to utilize "turning points" as a means to self-knowledge. Because Dostoevski both lived his problems and wrote about them, Wilson finds the "Outsider theme" dominating Dostoevski as an artist and as a man; and Wilson empathizes with many characters from Dostoevski's novels. The Russian writer obviously enjoyed analyzing criminals and psychopaths who *act*, and some of them are progenitors of Wilson's own fictional characters in later novels. Wilson particularly calls upon *The Brothers Karamazov* to demonstrate "The Great Synthesis," which is what he calls the major turning point in his own analysis.

According to Wilson, Dostoevski intended in *The Brothers Karamazov* to refute atheism. Ivan, whose case is critical, is seen as a superlative Outsider; for, as Wilson insists at this point in his argument, the Outsider's salvation "lies in extremes." His so-called way out comes to him in "visions, moments of intensity, etc." (202). As a matter of fact, the search for those "ways out" dominates most of Wilson's later works, especially his novels. For him the need to escape from triviality is a symptom of a disease which can provide its own cure in intensifying the symptoms. For example, an Outsider must, by his very nature, be restless and dissatisfied. When the Outsider fails, his failure is a personal tragedy, not merely a capitulation to things as they are. "Every Outsider tragedy we have studied so far," Wilson insists, "has been a tragedy of self-expression" (202) — the individual has been unable to express himself — unable not because fate, destiny, or matter has determined that incapacity, but because the individual has not yet potentiated the will to break through.

Wilson wholly endorses the advice of the poet William Blake: "Go and develop the visionary faculty" (246). In addition to Blake, Wilson calls upon the seventeenth-century English theologian and founder of the Society of Friends, George Fox, to whom he attributes the "strength of Will" to achieve insights far beyond the ordinary. Wilson praises both Blake and Fox for their resistance to those who regarded their visions as eccentric or insane. Wilson calls Fox, for example, "lucky" for being "able to do an apparently irrational thing without misgivings" (207). The point is that weak Outsiders, the kind Wilson calls "beetle-men," never get around to expressing themselves either rationally or irrationally.

Without agreeing with Fox's specifically religious pronouncements, Wilson praises the theologian for his attempts to understand. Before he died, however, Fox had become an Insider. After the delicate balance between insight and frustration was disturbed by Fox's wordly success, he acquired a smugness inimical to the true Outsider. In much the same way Wilson groups together D. H. Lawrence, Charles Dickens, Shaw, Wells, and Rainer Maria Rilke as men who began as Outsiders and who then exploited in their careers "that persistent desire towards self-discovery that made them all into major writers and intellectual driving-forces in their age" (218). They also, however, did not reach ultimate self-realization, because they all succeeded too soon and too easily. Ironically, an Outsider who fulfills his potential without struggling may cease to be an Outsider if he loses the continuing impulse toward further self-realization which is the essential characteristic of a true Outsider.

William Blake, however, remains exceptional; for he was never threatened with early success. Thus his struggles were always proportionate to his intensifying frustrations: the more he failed, the more he tried. Although luckier than Nietzsche in that he had a good wife, Blake saw the world much as the philosopher did; and he also resembled Rilke in that he endorsed "Yea-saying." As a visionary, Blake speaks eloquently for Wilson against "the rationalists and the 'natural religionists,' Gibbon, Voltaire, Rousseau, and the scientists Priestly and Newton" (236).

Among other Outsiders that interested Wilson in his omnivorous reading during his early years in the British Museum Reading Room, he includes several suicides. Although suicide is obviously not the way to *develop* the visionary faculty, suicide is an act of will. For those who have "exhausted the future," suicide can be a function of the liberating will rather than capitulation to despair. The Hindu yogi Ramakrishna, for example, found "ecstatic God-consciousness" (259) at the moment he killed himself. The fortitude of Christian saints in the face of certain death transcends ordinary suicide in a "fiery joy." Above all, however, in living or in dying, Wilson insists that "it is the Will that matters" (263).

George Gurdjieff and T. E. Hulme are the last two witnesses Wilson calls upon. Gurdjieff, who died in 1950, was a Caucasian Greek philosopher whom Wilson credits with finding "the complete, ideal Existenzphilosophie" (264). Despite Gurdjieff's weird belief that planetary bodies are alive, his methods for maximizing intensity interest Wilson; for men must be awakened. First, however, comes the awakening to the need to be awakened, which is a religious experience. Such subjectivity, although it is avowedly the only way to existential truth for Wilson, is nevertheless not to be allowed complete free play. "Religious truth," Wilson insists, "cannot exist apart from intellectual rigour, apart from the individual effort to realize it" (271); but Wilson's enthusiasm leads him into a dilemma: his own rejection of "mere intellect" is itself an intellectual act. He asks that subjective experience be analyzed objectively; but he cannot have his controls and transcend them too. Either his facts are provable, or they are not facts; and the scientific method is defensible as a method despite the tawdriness of much of its concerns.

Wilson struggles to resolve his dilemma. As he "swings the hammer," he is excited by the "intellectual questioning" of T. E. Hulme; and he refers to Kierkegaard's "revolt against Hegel" as a "philosophical stand against philosophy" (272). Both Wilson and Hulme are on the side of living. Protesting against the changes in existentialism made by Heidegger and Sartre, Wilson lines up with Hulme: "He is a poet, and his approach to religion is a poet's" (273). Because Hulme did not reject the possibility of a truly objective philosophy, he is useful to Wilson as one who pioneered what Wilson was hoping to perfect: a new philosophy which shows the way out of pessimism. Finally, Wilson insists "that the ideal 'objective philosophy' will not be constructed by mere thinkers, but by men who combine the thinker, the poet, and the man of action" (277). *The Outsider* ends quietly as Wilson admits the difficulties involved in making the effort to "see as a whole." Significantly, the last word of the book is "saint": "The individual begins that long effort as an Outsider; he may finish it as a saint" (281).

The Outsider was as extravagantly praised at first as it was extravagantly attacked later. The most curiously unpredictable aftermath of the appearance of *The Outsider* was the discovery that some supposedly informed writers were not really what they seemed. For example, Kingsley Amis in his review of the book admitted with striking candor that he thought most of the writers cited by Wilson had either been discredited long ago or were not worth knowing. Among those he himself had never heard of, or had dismissed as unimportant, he named Sartre, Camus, Kierkegaard, Nietzsche, Hesse, Hemingway, and Van Gogh! Amis also objected to the antirationalism of the work and felt that the attention paid to books about sickness is in itself a symptom of sickness.[5] All in all, he misunderstood the work, although he himself had written about the same kind of spiritual emptiness in his novel *Lucky Jim* (1954).

The acidulous *Times* reviewer concluded that the "charm of this book arises from its faults."[6] Indeed, Wilson's technique of casually juxtaposing his ideas and the ideas of others was faulty but it was also refreshing in that it stimulated new responses to familiar matter by providing unusual contexts. Wilson's lack of sophistication at the time he wrote *The Outsider* resulted in still other errors, such as abrupt transitions, laconic documentation or none at all, and *obiter dicta* which would have been avoided by more experienced writers on similar subjects, simply because they could have predicted that they would be challenged to prove the point. Young Wilson, however, could not have predicted such responses and thus was in good faith in his proud lack of fear of critical hostility. In fact, he never dreamed that his first book would be read by many, let alone be attacked or praised by famous critics and other serious contemporaries.

II Religion and the Rebel

Wilson's second philosophical work, *Religion and the Rebel,*[7] was published in 1957, hard on the heels of *The Outsider.* Although the young Truth-searcher again relies heavily upon his wide and often indiscriminate reading and again calls forth too many witnesses, he defines his terms more carefully than he does in *The Outsider.* In the course of the discussion, which again is alternately an argument in support of a thesis and an impassioned harangue, Wilson defends his first book and explicates some of his original assertions. In general, he orders his thoughts more neatly than in his first book. Structurally, *Religion and the Rebel* is divided into two parts. The first part, which contains a recapitulation of *The Outsider,* examines the decline of Western civilization; and the second part proposes certain resolutions and remedies. Jacob Bŏhme, Nicholas Ferrar, Blaise Pascal, Emanuel Swedenborg, William Law, John Henry Newman, Sŏren Kierkegaard, Bernard Shaw, Ludwig Wittgenstein, and Alfred North Whitehead testify as Outsiders whose various rebellions moved them toward an increased religious awareness.

The title of the work announces the topic of primary concern to the young philosopher at that time. *Religion and the Rebel* brings together and then defines the relationship between the Outsider's alienation and his religious appetite. Like *The Outsider,* the work is a kind of case book. The first group of witnesses Wilson calls upon include the "Outsider priest" from Shaw's *John Bull's Other Island;* the "Russian Hamlet who just cannot bring himself to do anything" from Ivan Goncharov's *Oblomov* (42); and various characters from the works of Samuel Beckett. Emphasizing the awareness in such Outsiders of the need for intensified consciousness, Wilson sees ruthlessness and crime as escapes from the tedium of mediocrity; and he also defends a special kind of deviation from so-called normal behavior as "supersanity." In Wilson's opinion, supersanity is the result of being extremely honest as well as above average in intelligence. Such awareness leads to "existence philosophy."

As an example of a supersane man, Wilson cites the German poet, Rainer Maria Rilke (1875 - 1926). Although he finds Rilke's famous *Malte Laurids Brigge* "one of the gloomiest books ever written" (53), he praises Rilke for his extraordinary will power. In summarizing Rilke's significance, however, Wilson insists that Rilke ended as a failure; for he did not transcend his creations: "Rilke synthesized his experience for the purpose of art, not for the purpose of wider and deeper experience" (67). It is obvious by this time that Wilson as philosopher and critic is inexorable in his demands. Again, as when evaluating George Fox in *The Outsider,* Wilson reveals his conviction that ultimate success can corrupt original integrity and that, unless the critic judges the total impact of a creator *and* his creations, he is being superficial.

Wilson next evaluates the significance of the French symbolist poet Arthur Rimbaud (1854 - 91), whose importance lies in his championing the imagination. He speaks for the Outsider who makes "war on his rationality" (79). Although Wilson compares him with William Blake in his rejection of reason, Rimbaud unfortunately failed when his visions faded: "He began by thinking of himself as a god; he ended by thinking of himself as human. That was his tragedy" (80). The American novelist F. Scott Fitzgerald also failed, because he was "paid and flattered by the age" for informing others that everyone is sensitive (91). Crisply defining his own kind of existentialism as "the revolt against mere logic and reason" (99), Wilson dismisses Fitzgerald and calls upon the German philosopher Oswald Spengler (1880 - 1936) to support Wilson's emphasis on intuition and other nonrational perceptions in the revolt against "mere thinking." Although Spengler's work is "monstrously badly written" (100) and although his ultimate fatalism is too pessimistic, Wilson endorses Spengler's cyclical vision of history and also admires the man-in-action aspects of Spengler, his daring and his nonconformity.

Among the predecessors and contemporaries of Spengler who interest Wilson for approximately the same reasons, he cites Giambattista Vico, Pierre Ballanche, Henry Adams, George Sorel, Vilfredo Pareto, Jacob Burckhardt, Nicholas Danilevsky, and particularly the English historian Arnold Toynbee, who addressed himself to history in ways compatible with the Outsider's experience of reality. Praising Toynbee for his "hostility to pedantry," an attitude for which critics had also faulted Wilson, Wilson emphathizes with Toynbee's rejection of the scientific method. The accuracy or inaccuracy of Wilson's interpretation of Toynbee, however, is of minor concern here; for Wilson insists on nothing more than the validity of the *spirit* of his own inquiry into the *spirit* of Toynbee's analyses.[8] Indeed, doubt concerning the ultimate validity of Spengler's conclusions is dismissed by Wilson as "only another example of the hostility of mere academics to any work of creative imagination that trespasses on their domain of 'fact' " (117).

After comparing Toynbee with novelist-philosopher Aldous Huxley, who had also eventually acknowledged the function of religion in history, Wilson announces the major theme of this second volume, namely, the motivation and direction of the Outsider's rebellion as a religious act. Stressing the similarities between the teachings of Christ, Nietzsche, and Buddha, Wilson speculates that his kind of Outsider *could* have used the church by turning-on his "spiritual energy" in constructive ways. Things went wrong, however; the Outsider's anarchism became his glory; and his commitments were inevitably incompatible with institutionalized religion. The most famous of the Outsider-apostates, or rebels, whom Wilson cites to bolster his case include the heretics Peter Waldo, John Wycliffe, John Huss, and Martin Luther, as well as the innovators Nicolaus Copernicus, Giordano Bruno, Galileo, and René Descartes.

At this point in his argument, Wilson tries to disentangle his concerns. First, he insists that the Outsider is an existentialist. Because he insists that the Outsider's existentialism is basically religious, he feels it necessary to distinguish hurriedly between good religion and bad religion and between Christ and Paul. Rejecting the simplistic methods of psychoanalysis and communism, as well as the pretentious methods of science and Christian theology, he specifically denounces both polar extremes: "To the Outsider, the *Weltanschauung* of the scientists is as absurd and oversimplified as the Weltanschauung of the Church"(148). He thus throws the responsibility upon each individual to discover for himself his capacity to change himself — if he so *wills*.

To the existentialist, man is born with some ability to change as well as to resist alteration; and this flexibility and resilience Wilson tries not to confuse with sentimentalized freedom. He insists that his objective in *The Outsider* has been to prove that the humanist claim that man is born free is "rubbish": "Man is not born free; he is born in chains that are far more degrading and demoralizing than loss of social liberty: the chains of boredom and futility. Without a discipline to give him purpose and save him from his own aimlessness, man is nothing" (132). Refinements in Wilson's theory in subsequent essays and novels gloss these problems, but essentially Wilson at this time had identified the coordinates of his philosophical position. His ultimates are both mystical and heroic. Over and over again he insists that a man *can* achieve if he *wills* to do so. Disaffected by the dullness of most people and sick of the venality of those who are bright enough to reject dullness but not heroic enough to reject venality, Wilson exalts the potential for significance in a small but important segment of humanity.

Among those whom he calls "teachers of the reality of the Will," Wilson names Jacob Böhme, Nicholas Ferrar, Blaise Pascal, and Emanuel Swedenborg (208). "There is about these men," he says, "some enormous strength that does not require the acknowledgement and recognition of the outside world. This is the sign of the true mystic" (150); and this sign Wilson now searches for. Few of the witnesses in his first work were mystics, but Wilson now defines the Outsider as "the man who strives to become a mystic" (151). Noting that he is "definitely abandoning the whole viewpoint of the Insider," he announces his new program as a "plunge into the depths of the Outsider's inner-world" (151).

Man's "inner-world" is traditionally studied by both theologians and psychologists. Certain psychologists, such as the American B. F. Skinner, are said to have emptied the human organism of all content, especially of the mind and of the soul, in order to concentrate their study on the observable aspects of a person's behavior. Obviously they were soon called behaviorists by both their admirers and their enemies — the latter used the term pejoratively, of course, implying *mere* behaviorism. Colin Wilson rejects behaviorism, preferring the assumption that not all important psychological facts are observable. He admires Böhme's definition of psychology as "the anatomy of the soul" (161). Furthermore, in his eagerness to support his own ideas, Wilson links together such improbable associates as Böhme, Nietzsche, Rimbaud, and Shaw — all of whom, he contends, were searching for the nature of reality by cultivating visions, the importance of which is central to man's search for self-realization: "Having a 'vision' is like being connected with a powerhouse; floods of energy and vitality sluice into the brain, and the brain lights up, like a mansion in which every light in every room has been turned on. This is the ecstasy of self-knowledge" (167).

Nicholas Ferrar, an English theologian born in 1592, is also cited as an Outsider who turned his back on the world. Admittedly, Wilson cannot classify Ferrar as a true mystic; but he wants him among his witnesses for the relevance of his experimental community, Little Gidding, in which gentleness, sharing and worship were supposed to dominate. "Nicholas Ferrar," Wilson notes with some nostalgia for the innocence of Ferrar's utopian project, "had chosen one way out of the Outsider's dilemma; he had set his own little corner of the world in order, and lived in that corner as if the rest of the world did not exist" (175). Yet Wilson objects to the surrendering of reason required in such a solution.

Although the Outsider, as a rebel, must transcend logic, perhaps even sanity, he must not at the same time give up his "intellectual rigour." Wilson's Outsider is always intelligent. His resistance to surrendering to either despair or materialism is thoughtful. Systematic attempts, such as socialism, to decrease human suffering by increasing controls must also be rejected. The Outsider is a lonely hero.

Wilson's admiration for the French mathematician and philosopher Blaise Pascal relates to his own identification with this versatile but disciplined rebel. Wilson discusses Pascal's achievements as an Outsider, particularly his espousal of Jansenism, the heresy which emphasizes God's predestination as limiting atonement for even the best of human beings. Wilson's praise of Pascal's conversion to Jansenism is not a blanket approval of his heresy as much as an enthusiastic response to Pascal's own willfulness, for Jansen's conviction that man can do nothing to win God's grace is contrary to Wilson's emphasis on free will. Yet, just as Pascal made of this stalemate between God and man grounds for attacking humanism and atheism, Wilson uses Pascal's Outsiderism as an occasion to support his own outrageousness. In other words, the heroism of Pascal is more important to Wilson than the ultimate validity of his ideas.

Wilson hammers away at his point again and again: "Do not ask whether the philosophy is true; look at the philosopher and ask whether he is great. A man who is not obsessed cannot be great" (190). Just as Pascal surpassed smaller figures in sweep and scope, so Swedenborg surpassed the "cranky messiahs" (198). His trances were built on a large scale, he visited heaven and hell, and he reported many conversations with angels. Although Wilson does not accept these reports as factual, he does again defend visions per se as high imagination and thus as a means to knowledge. The significance of Swedenborg, of course, for Wilson's purposes, must be referred to the whole man rather than to specific teachings. While emphasizing the importance of emotions, Wilson does not insist that the wise man can rely solely upon his feelings or his visions; and Wilson's respect for skepticism pushes him into a compromise. Noting that skepticism must question emotions as well as logic, Wilson concludes that the ideal philosophy would combine reliance on visions with intellectual skepticism concerning those visions. Certainly the prescription is rather ingenuously stated despite the good faith which underlies Wilson's quest for Truth!

The next two witnesses, the devotional writer William Law and the theologian John Henry Newman, are relatively respectable, Wilson realizes, in that neither reported visions nor scandalized society in other ways. Although they were thus not completely Outsiders, their teachings are relevant to the Outsider's problems. Like Shaw and Nietzsche, Law exhorted man to utilize many of his powers that were as yet untested. Also, Wilson endorses Law's proper use of his intellectual power: "He was religious in the most essential meaning of the word: not out of any emotional need or human weakness, but out of sheer strength; the craving of a powerful mind and vital will for still greater health, and deeper consciousness and vitality" (218). Law had everything Wilson admires except visions. Similarly, Cardinal Newman, although deeply religious, had few ecstatic experiences. Although Newman anticipated existentialism in his rejection of formal logic, Wilson applauds the nobility of Newman's personal life more than he does his teachings. "If the twentieth century could produce even a few men of Newman's stature," Wilson notes, "the whole course of history might be changed" (231).

In contrast to his qualified but real enthusiasm for Law and Newman, Wilson is much cooler in his approach to the Danish theologian Sören Kierkegaard. Perhaps Wilson could not help reacting negatively to the growing popularity of the nineteenth-century father of existentialism. Wilson claims that Kierkegaard had disproportionately emphasized his personal anguish, and he refuses to acknowledge Kierkegaard's seminal importance. Admitting that Kierkegaard had defined chaos, Wilson almost petulantly faults the theologian for not dealing with his "suffering unto death" more courageously.

George Bernard Shaw, however, qualifies for the highest honors on all counts in Wilson's hierarchy. The young philosopher's admiration for the recalcitrant dramatist, who had died only a few years before, approaches idolatry. Claiming Shaw to be equal in importance to Augustine and Aquinas, Wilson sees in the man and his works the true marks of the Outsider. He makes Shaw the third in a holy trio of which the first two are Plato and Goethe, but he also ranks Shaw with H. G. Wells. All these men, Wilson contends, were "thinkers for whom thought and life are inseparable" (243). However, he particularly exalts Shaw, calling him "the key figure of existentialist thought" (289) as he traces the theme of the Outsider in Shaw's development as a writer. The demonstration points to the existence of a dominating hunger for heroism and religion in the Outsider. But religion is not to be defined carelessly. A desirable religious consciousness comes with discipline. Shaw's definition of self-control is accepted by Wilson as a definition of religion: "a highly developed vital sense, dominating and regulating the mere appetites" (278). Some dozen years later Wilson expanded this thesis into a book-length "reassessment" of Shaw.[9]

Wilson climaxes his arguments in *Religion and the Rebel* with support from the Viennese-born philosopher Ludwig Wittgenstein, and the English mathematician Alfred North Whitehead. The ideas of the former, for Wilson's purposes, imply a mysticism which the ideas of the latter make explicit. Defending his own interpretation of Wittgenstein's significance, Wilson asserts that the philosopher himself "did not fully understand the implications of his own book." For Wilson, Wittgenstein's *Tractatus* was a revolt against Bertrand Russell and the self-sufficiency of logic, and also a challenge to those philosophers whose positivism underwrites contemporary physical science and psychological behaviorism. Again and again Wilson insists that "true existentialism cannot be communicated in ordinary logical language" (301). Wittgenstein almost made it, Wilson concedes, but he should have written a novel like *Brothers Karamazov* — "to discipline himself until he achieved *samadhi* like Ramakrishna" (302).

Whitehead is a less equivocal witness for the defense. Rejecting scientific materialism for its omission of man's free will, Whitehead pleased Wilson and others antagonistic to the assumption of positivism, which Wilson defines as "a kind of Marxist materialism" (293), when he quite dogmatically announced that "the poets are right, and the scientists are wrong" (309). Wilson equates his own aims in his philosophical analyses with Whitehead's: "Both views begin with a rejection of scientific materialism (and its natural rejection of religion) and an appeal to the psychological foundations of common sense" (309). Of central importance is Whitehead's idea of "prehension," which is dramatically defined by Wilson, following Whitehead's specifications, as "that act of the soul, reaching out like an octopus to digest its experience" (310). Fixing on "prehension" as the basic act in existentialism, an act carefully to be distinguished from "apprehension," which is based on *intellectual* rather than *soulful* understanding, Wilson rests his own case. Having derived his highest good, as Whitehead did, from the inadequacy of apprehensions which do not boldly and honestly face chaos, Wilson audaciously vows to take up where Whitehead left off.

Religion and the Rebel presents the case for rebellion as a religious experience. The Outsider has certain prerequisites for religious experience, but he must outface the chaos his rebellion uncovers. Wittgenstein ended as "creator manqué" because he failed to "prehend" deeply enough. Without embarrassment, for Wilson is still young and passionately involved in his quest, he can now assert the following, believing sincerely that he has defined his terms and supported his position: "A man becomes great in so far as he expresses the will of God, which is an eternal act of prehension in life" (312).

Critical opinion of this second volume in the Outsider series was generally harsh although often fair in attacking the *obiter dicta* and redundancies — qualities which are perhaps attenuated in this abbreviated summary of the work. It is difficult not to betray Wilson's excitement, his most appealing characteristic in his early works, by reducing his arguments to a more pedestrian kind of sense than he intended. As he himself has argued with reference to those writers he admires most: it is the man who finally counts. The better part of critical judgment requires patience with apprentices and initiation.

One otherwise hostile critic admitted that "in the unabashed conceit and pugnacious ignorance of the book, Mr. Wilson may well be, as he claims, a portent."[10] Citing Wilson's frenzied vehemence or his brash self-confidence as simultaneously both negative and positive traits, other critics fell in line with the ambiguous verdict on the work. In fact, Wilson's own Outsiders would expect such treatment, which in turn would stiffen their resistance and thus make them even more intensely Outsiders.

Wilson's effort to arouse an apparently indifferent society and to liberate his oppressed Outsiders was characterized by critics in the same breath as lucid and sententious, as flamboyant and erudite. Wilson was called a false prophet and an honest man, and other such improbable pairs of epithets. He was denounced as an upstart and at the same time praised for daring to be one. Typical of this kind of ambivalence is the following evaluation by Robert Peel, which appeared in a sedate American newspaper: "However bizarre Mr. Wilson's adolescent thrashings around may have been and however annoying his later posturings, there is an essential dignity in his purpose."[11]

Colin Wilson continued to survive both the cleverness and the hostility of reviewers and critics, and he plunged on.

III The Stature of Man

Implicit in the faith in human progress is the assumption that humans are capable of *significant* behavior. After that assumption has been accepted, it is then one easy step to the next assumption that some humans are capable of *heroic* behavior. In *The Stature of Man* (1959),[12] the third book concerned with the Outsider, Wilson exalts the "heroic urge" as "the desire of life to find a broader field for its powers" (165). The book is a call to bear arms in a cultural revolution to be led by existential thinkers. Once more Wilson relies heavily on articulate witnesses, a group selected this time to testify specifically in support of "the new existentialism as a mystical revolt, based upon recognition of the irrational urge that underlies man's conscious reason" (158).

The witnesses who interest Wilson the most in this volume are those who willfully promote some kind of significance. Wilson himself takes an heroic stand against what he calls the "insignificance fallacy," the tendency to exalt failure as a good. He resists the antihero and the other manifestations of the pathetic modern temper which have debased courage and discipline as neurotic weaknesses or as mere words. Calling for the rejection of current fashions in despair and nihilism, Wilson turns to the "evidence of sociology" and then to the "evidence of literature" to establish the sad fact that heroism has vanished. He first cites David Riesman's *The Lonely Crowd* and William Whyte's *The Organization Man*, but he also draws examples from the writings of Vance Packard, J. D. Galbraith, Frederick Wertham, and Harrison Salisbury, all of whom agree, after making allowances for vocabulary differences, that "other-directedness" is prevalent and undesirable in both America and England. Socially conditioned beings obey the ways of the community, and Outsiders are penalized.

Wilson also sees the "revolts" of the protagonists in American and British novels as primarily other-directed, that is, as conforming to conventionalized patterns of rebellion, rather than as inner-directed and individualized. Thus he is dissatisfied with the fiction of Kingsley Amis, John Wain, and John Osborne, the so-called Angry Young Men. By the same token he objects to those American novelists who glorify defeat such as William Faulkner, John Dos Passos and Ernest Hemingway. For example, he says of Faulkner: "He admires, in the modern world, minor, unheroic figures who 'endure' like Lena Grove in *Light in August* and Dilsey in *The Sound and the Fury*. There is no heroism left" (45). The Beat generation, especially the San Francisco school, Wilson finds more vigorous at least than their elders, but again he brands their respective revolts as too reflexive and as too predictable. Of most twentieth-century American literature, including the plays of Tennessee Williams, Arthur Miller, and Elmer Rice, Wilson concludes that "the individual is reduced to a cipher to be defeated and crushed . . ." (54).

Obviously, Wilson is pleading his special cause with these sweeping indictments of writers whose concerns and commitments are usually more subtle than Wilson credits; but, all in all, the various writers are not so casually dismissed as this summary must perforce make it seem. Passing tributes to the purely literary skills, even genius, of each writer indicate that Wilson is not deaf or blind to literature. Eager to defeat defeatism, Wilson is, however, frequently guilty of reducing American novels in particular to philosophical statements about the human condition; and he is almost equally harsh in his judgments on English novelists. He is impatient with Angus Wilson's failure to exalt heroic qualities without hedging Wilson wants real anger rather than the superficial antics of a character like Amis's hero in *Lucky Jim*, who is an example of "Riesman's other-directed man with a veneer of rebelliousness" (61).

In an attempt to identify the dynamics of authentic heroism, Wilson exalts anyone who defies the *status quo*. A host of proper heroes from the old days are contrasted with effete moderns as Wilson traces the evolution of the Faustian hero through several stages of deterioration until he has descended to "the ordinary chap" of this era. Surprisingly, Wilson finds the beginnings of the decline of heroism in the works of Charles Dickens, Honoré Balzac, Gustave Flaubert, Ivan Turgenev, and George Eliot. Taking in gigantic gulps of literature, as if he were a runner out of breath having difficulty drawing in air, Wilson rejects Emile Zola as deficient in imagination; and he indicts D. H. Lawrence, Evelyn Waugh, and Graham Greene as specializing in a "type of literary confidence trick" which "depends on the reader's not possessing enough imagination to envisage a higher destiny for the hero . . . than the one the author has selected for him — collective farming, the Catholic church, or being Lady Chatterley's lover" (99). Although Wilson praises the protagonist in Robert Musil's *The Man Without Qualities*, Wilson despises Proust's Marcel for his personal weaknesses. And he dismisses all of Thomas Mann's work except the tetralogy, *Joseph and His Brothers*, which he approves of because Joseph appears as an authentic hero.

Wilson's existentialism is obviously vested with his own concerns, namely, the rehabilitation of humanity. Insofar as heroism is most clearly revealed in heroic *actions*, existential psychology increasingly interests Wilson and provides him with justifications for his impatience with Sartre and Camus. Only that "awful freedom" which a man feels when confronted with the indifference of the universe can, according to Sartre and Camus, make a man brave. Wilson disagrees, for he refuses to correlate freedom and terror: "Freedom is not merely terror; it is any intense emotion that restores a man's subjectivity" (118). Thus Wilson prepares the case for the desirability of increasing the duration as well as the frequency of liberating experiences.

In the last sections of *The Stature of Man*, Wilson clearly formulates what for him is the big question of our time: "Is it possible for existentialism to become something more positive?" (133). Calling for a war on insignificance, he asks for the restoration of heroism as the proper measure of man. Above all, he feels that the artist must create the new hero, while the philosopher must add his support to the program. The imperative is clear: "As a philosophy, existentialism must emphasize the primacy of the will, the importance of the individual, the final unpredictability and freedom of even the most neurotic and conditioned human being." And then Wilson adds, with a modesty that hostile critics have overlooked: "The real work still remains to be done; these comments are only attempts to foresee its direction" (160).

Edmund Fuller called *The Stature of Man* Wilson's "best book" to date partly because it was the shortest. Less facetiously, however, Fuller praised the work for its clear focus. He also allowed that Wilson's "critique of the inadequacy of modern thinking and characterization" was "trenchant," but he deplored the young philosopher's "conclusions."[13] Irving Howe indicted the work as a "smorgasbord for the half-educated, passing off sloppiness of thought as creative synthesis."[14] Robert Peel called Wilson "a brash, bookish, rather muddled young man with not very much talent for writing and not very much precision in thinking . . ."and then went on to admit his own "respect" for the writer's "honesty of attention and some of the insights at which he arrives."[15] These relatively gentle responses were from American critics. On the British side of the ocean, however, the massacre of the young upstart was now at its bloodiest. "Mr. Wilson has gone in for ideas," the anonymous *Times* reviewer sneered, then zoomed in for the kill: "His mind has not yet, so far as may be judged from his public utterances, generated an original idea, even of the demonstrably false variety which most other young men's minds generate in profusion."[16]

The writing of *The Stature of Man* was cathartic for the young author. His ideas were certainly not all brand new, but his emphasis on the accountability of literature in a moral context defied the aesthetic purity of the aging New Criticism still practiced by the followers of T. S. Eliot. Wilson's argument concludes with a statement which both recapitulates the thesis of the book and predicts the directions of Wilson's own writing: "The responsibility of literature in the twentieth century becomes appallingly clear: to illuminate man's freedom" (171). The harsh responses to his good intentions reinforced his determination to continue his mission not only to illuminate man's freedom in his novels but also to evaluate in his critical writings the relative success and failure of others.

CHAPTER 3

The Outsider as Philosopher: II

I The Strength to Dream

WITH the fourth volume in the Outsider cycle, *The Strength to Dream* (1962),[1] Wilson's project begins to take on the dimensions of a systematic philosophy. No less urgent but more deliberate, Wilson cites both central tendencies and deviations — he uses whatever he finds as either positive or negative evidence to support his thesis. That which tends to support his hypothesis, *his* norm, is correct; that which goes contrary to, or moves away from, his norm is incorrect. However, correctness and incorrectness are both valuable witnesses, for as many inferences can be drawn from the blunders of the dull as from the insights of the bright when what is at issue is the *difference* between dullness and brightness, between seeing clearly and seeing dimly.

Polarities activate the imagination. Aldous Huxley in *Point Counterpoint* recognized the healthy stimulation that comes from pitting passion against reason. The need for such clashes, with sound and fury signifying something, is an article of faith with Wilson. For him, passionate value judgments are vitalisms. An example of one of his highly emotive judgments about literary values is Wilson's insistence that good literature must be moral, since it is always concerned with the *how* of living: "No matter how detached and uncommitted an artist pretends to be, he is involved in a world whose 'direction' is as positive as the current of a river. It is impossible to exercise the imagination and not to be involved in this current, in man's need for a supra-personal purpose, in the evolutionary drive" (207).

Imagination, for Wilson, must include a special kind of vision — a liberated vision in which the liberation may be both an asset and a liability as it explores unknown lands and as it swings wide in its surveys and reports. What Wilson calls the "social realist" definition of imagination offers only carbon copies of reality; for it points too often in the direction of romantic escapism and compensation, toward trivial dreams and trivial solutions. Wilson insists that the kind of imagination which he has *inferred* from inadequate manifestations and from imprecisions (the *true* imagination, the kind that could liberate the Outsider from his isolation) must always refer itself to the big issues, such as the meaning of existence. To achieve even a beginning toward such a liberating vision, the writer must stand back from immediate concerns and relate to the flux of experience. He must be careful, however, not to be submerged by that flux. Allegedly this kind of imagination is a third dimension of consciousness, of which the other two dimensions are simple awareness and memory. In its most intensified form, in which the third dimension is working harmoniously with the other two dimensions, the imagination becomes a "detonator of the will" (190): "Imagination is man's attempt to break out of the prison of his body, to possess an extension beyond the present" (195).

Throughout *The Strength to Dream,* Wilson seeks to define this imaginative factor. He organizes six groups of witnesses from whom he quotes, paraphrases, and infers evidence to support his own convictions about the nature and importance of imagination. The first group shares a common characteristic, namely, the "assault on rationality." The second and third groups are classified, respectively, according to "the implications of realism" and "the implications of total pessimism." Members of the fourth group have shared "the vision of science," particularly those visions which project a better future life. The fifth group has shared "the powers of darkness," and the sixth group has speculated on the relationship between "sex and the imagination." Wilson's own conclusions about the imagination compose a final chapter in which "the need for polarities" is analyzed and defended. The organization of the book is arbitrary, the categories are not mutually exclusive, and the overall effect is more dramatic than logical. It is all, however, predictably enthusiastic.

Wilson begins by praising H. P. Lovecraft, a writer "of dubious genius" who died in 1937 at the age of forty-seven. Lovecraft's many fantasy-novels have founded a cult similar to, but much smaller than, that inspired by J. R. R. Tolkien. Much influenced by Edgar Allan Poe, Lovecraft had never before been compared with John Keats for his "war with rationality" or with Peter Kürten, a murderer who specialized in his sexual sadistic fantasies (1 - 2). After this unexpected resurrection of Lovecraft, an admittedly bad writer, Wilson compares the poetic visions of Yeats with the theories of George Gurdjieff, the mad philosopher who had claimed that the universe itself is alive. He also praises the dramatists Oscar Wilde and August Strindberg for their more or less successful escape from tedium into imaginative madness and then their subsequent return to an improved normalcy, a healthier modality purified by the assault they had sustained on mere rationality.[2]

Among those who demonstrate the "implications" — the uses and abuses of "realism" — Zola is charged with sensationalism at its commercial worst. Nathanael West comes off better, but only because he wrote more competently, not because he had anything more significant to say; for Wilson accuses him of a paralyzed imagination and downgrades him along with William Faulkner, Graham Greene, and Evelyn Waugh. He finds William Faulkner guilty of affectation, Evelyn Waugh of "Catholic snobbery" (45), and Graham Greene of being "too close to the 'pain threshold' " (52). Indicting these writers for failing to ameliorate the evils of that reality they claim to mirror in their novels, Wilson admits his preference for classifying novelists as optimists or rejectors rather than as romantics or classicists. Above all, he insists that the writer fulfill the promises he makes to the reader, no matter which category he is in. Rejecting the classification of literary works into genres, Wilson levies responsibility on each piece of literature to deal honestly with the human condition. In temperament, Wilson resembles impatient Marxists who have been trained to test literature for political validity only. Of course, Wilson is far from a Marxist in his humanistic convictions, but he does demand his kind of authenticity from each work of art as well as from each artist.

Wilson admires discipline, and for this attribute he respects hardworkers like Sartre, Shaw, and Nietzsche. He praises Sartre for not taking the easy way; yet he completely rejects Sartre's defeatism, as he sees it. Among those experimenting with the so-called antinovel, Wilson disapproves of both Nathalie Sarraute and Alain Robbe-Grillet; he concludes that they have been too preoccupied with techniques rather than with ideas. He responds positively to the rebelliousness per se in such innovators, but he does not accept the validity of the technical products of that rebellion. Their novels lack ideological vitality.

The next group whom Wilson accuses of total pessimism includes Leonid Andreyev and Samuel Beckett. He disagrees with their messages while admiring their courage in declaring themselves. Differentiating between morality and aesthetics, Wilson also believes he has differentiated between the good uses and the abuses of the imagination. Such a bifurcation makes it possible for him to deal seriously with aesthetic trivia as he searches for the key to what he calls "the crisis in modern literature" (xi - xxiv). As part of his quest, he turns logically enough to the traditional Utopias and anti-Utopias for evidence of the stimulating effect of science on the imagination. He honors H. G. Wells once again as a great writer and acknowledges the importance of Eugene Zamiatin's *We*. He concludes that, at its best, science fiction can be vital in its high inventiveness. Probing "The Power of Darkness," he pairs such dissimilar writers as de Sade and Tolkien. James Joyce is placed in the same category with Gothic novelists like Sheridan Le Fanu, M. R. James, Algernon Blackwood, Sergei Aksakov, and E. T. Hoffman. Relative to the others in this arbitrarily formed category, Wilson judges the writing of Joyce as nonheroic. The verdict is obviously, however, a function of the category. In truth, Wilson is not very comfortable with the works of Joyce, particularly with *Ulysses* and *Finnegans Wake*, for he has trouble classifying these novels.

Wilson is more confident as he moves on to his next group, "Sex and the Imagination." There he finds the scandalous Frenchman de Sade more limited in imagination than William Blake. Blake, Wilson insists, knew more about sex. For one thing, he knew that sex was a potent stimulus for the imagination, as did several writers less notorious than de Sade, such as the French short-story writer Guy de Maupassant; the German dramatist Frank Wedekind; the Russian novelist Mikhail P. Artzybasheff; and the British novelist D. H. Lawrence. Because Maupassant "accepted all experience without analysis," he is impatiently labeled "the most completely brainless of all the great authors" (163). In contrast, Wedekind is praised for the skill with which he intertwined crime and sex in his plays; the little-known Artzybasheff is exalted for his Blakean-Nietzschean novel, *Sanine;* and D. H. Lawrence is disqualified as "too small a man to be a satisfactory instrument of the vision that sometimes possessed him" (186).

Such judgments, although supported by more evidence than can be cited here, are often eccentric in the real sense of the word. They are off-center. At best, they provoke interest; at worst, they are grotesque. The fact that Wilson often disagrees with established assessments is not in itself disturbing. There is a real possibility, however, that such *total* judgments are anathema to someone else who may be equally in good faith. Colin Wilson has infuriated those who prefer a fine reading of a literary text to the so-called existential impact of that text on all humanity.

Agreeing with Wilson's thesis that many modern writers have been "mistaking personal whiffiness for objective truth," Benjamin De Mott, a hard-hitting American critic, endorsed Wilson's objective while deploring his "boyish impatience with the world as it looks to plain, non-Platonic men."[3] A British critic approved of Wilson but disliked the book for doing "less than justice to Mr. Wilson's intellectual powers, his seriousness, originality, and sensibility."[4] Another reviewer lamented Wilson's "frequent unawareness that he is not the first in the field," and then added the familiar qualification: "These giant oversimplifications are attractively fresh and enthusiastic. . . . "[5]

Wilson's "oversimplifications," however, were never meant to be "a fair substitute for criticism." Wilson's enthusiasm sometimes encourages hasty speculations and sweeping judgments, but he has insisted all along that he is not a *mere* critic and thus should not be judged in that category. It is ultimately as a philosopher that he must be judged either significant or not. Time and work are of the essence — and on his side.

II Origins of the Sexual Impulse

In *Origins of the Sexual Impulse* (1963),[6] the fifth volume of the Outsider cycle, the maturing Wilson begins to rely more on his own experience and to cite authorities less often. He is also certain now that he is pushing forward the frontiers of knowledge. In this volume Wilson confidently promises to explain sexuality and to ascertain what roles the sexual impulse takes "in man's total being." He announces first of all that he accepts the assertions of the "science of phenomenology" and "form-psychology" as "facts." He then brings his own intuitions in line with these facts, acknowledging his indebtedness to Edmund Husserl, who is usually regarded as the founder of modern phenomenology, as well as to the Gestaltists or form-psychologists. Both phenomenologists and Gestaltists have argued that human perception is a process which does not yield its secrets to scientists who confine their research to dissecting and atomizing. Wilson also prefers the kinds of psychology and philosophy which speculate about the "unconscious" and other mysteries, such as extrasensory perception. Wilson argues that the "filters" between man and reality which help preserve sanity, as it is defined by the community, also impose "a certain sameness on our days, a sameness that is the opposite of the 'visionary gleam' " (66).

In support of his belief that potentiated man must avoid such simplistic behavior as conforming with others merely to avoid conflict with mediocrity, Wilson is once again on familiar ground and calls upon some familiar witnesses. This time, however, the emphasis shifts to sexuality; for, to Wilson, the sexual impulse in humans is a special instinct that must be carefully differentiated from the mating behavior of animals. He defends human sexuality as "the shortest and easiest route" to achieve "heightened consciousness" (28). In passing, Wilson evaluates the variations of the "Casanova impulse" described by the pornographer Frank Harris, who had learned to use sexual conquest to bolster self-respect, and by the avant-garde novelist Henry Miller, whose sexual athleticism Wilson treats with tolerance and appreciation but whose existential significance Wilson faults because of Miller's confused values. Determined to understand the processes at work in these prodigious lovers and to find the common denominator in sexuality, Wilson rejects traditional norms. His attitude toward all so-called deviations is permissive as he searches for the individual's intentions as revealed in sex acts. To phenomenologists, "intentionality" is the significant variable; for one does what one intends to do. Conditioned, reflexive behavior is primitive and sub-human.

The sexual act for Wilson is never reflexive. "The sexual orgasm is a response to an act of will and imagination rather than to a physical reality" (59). Tying together Gestalt psychology and phenomenological method, Wilson focuses on the individual's own perception of what he is doing. Since he believes that man is free to make choices, he asks him to choose increased awareness in his sexual acts. He recommends that one willfully minimize one's filtering out of reality. How? "The easiest means of achieving an immediate broadening of consciousness," Wilson answers, "is the sexual orgasm" (69).

Sexuality is the one dimension which everyone, privileged and underprivileged, acknowledges as a problem. In other areas of human concerns, the villainous limitation of consciousness is not so readily perceived. Wilson is convinced that sexual activity suffers more than any other human behavior from willful distortions. Measuring the extent of such distortions from his assumed norm, he breaks with the Freudian tradition decisively when he stresses the positive value of abnormalities such as superconsciousness and supersexuality. He advocates excess rather than parsimony: "Sex, like alcohol," he says, "has the capacity to destroy . . . stagnation; to turn the consciousness of ourselves into a Niagara" (91).

Certainly de Sade avoided stagnation whatever other harms he may have inflicted on himself and on others. Recklessly, Wilson asserts that "there is not one of us in whom de Sade's quest for total and final fulfillment does not arouse a certain sympathy" (95). Recognizing that, biologically, sex acts imply reproduction, Wilson nevertheless gives humans the right to use sex for nonreproductive functions. When Wilson exhorts the half-dead to arise from lethargy, to choose and to enjoy satisfying sexual intercourse, he is doing something more important than condoning sexual frankness. He is justifying sex existentially; that is, he believes sex is not only biological but also *intentional*, man's free and liberating choice.

Origins of the Sexual Impulse was dubbed the "poor man's Kraft-Ebbing."[7] As such it was variously misread by those whose orthodoxy was offended. For example, Wilson was accused of "scrapping Freudian theory along with the moral boundaries that traditionally defined sex as normal or abnormal, right or wrong. . . ."[8] Eric Moon, in *The Library Journal*, advised against adding the book "to any except the most bullet-proof and daring of general collections in public libraries."[9] Obviously, Wilson's effect on tender sensibilities had not diminished by 1963. After all, had not the great Freud relegated sex to a comfortably unconscious area of human concerns? Had he not also approved of the suppression of sexual impulses as a means of motivating creativity via sublimation? Freud was the true prophet, but Wilson was a heretic! Today's heresies, however, often become tomorrow's truths. Wilson begins to find comfort in being a heretic, for did not his heresy predict that he might become tomorrow's true prophet? He went back to work more eagerly than ever.

III Beyond the Outsider

Subtitled *The Philosophy of the Future, Beyond the Outsider* (1965)[10] is the sixth and final volume in the Outsider cycle. By this time, Wilson claims for each member of the series "that it is impossible for any one of them to be fully understood without the others" (11); but, for this book in particular, Wilson asks maximum respect, noting that he revised it several times before he allowed it to be published. By now, however, Wilson's battle cries are becoming familiar: Man must assert himself! Man can know what there is to know! Man must not succumb to despair! Any action is preferred to lethargy! Even pain can lower the threshold of awareness and thus help dispel indifference!

That "margin of human consciousness that can be stimulated by pain, but not by pleasure" (30) has to do with the gap between high and low vitality.[11] Indifference is the result of stimulation's not reaching the person; instead, it raises the so-called threshold and blocks much desirable experience. Wilson estimates that up to 95 percent of his fellow humans are victims of indifference, and to arouse these dulled awarenesses it is necessary either to increase the strength of the stimuli to which they are exposed or to alter their thresholds downward. Since the so-called doors of perception are not firmly closed, Wilson exhorts men to *will* themselves into responsiveness. Although, like Aldous Huxley and others, he had experimented with drugs as "door-openers," Wilson prefers persuasion and exhortation.

In his defense, Wilson again calls on H. G. Wells to testify. Claiming that Wells had prophetic knowledge of the later discoveries of existentialists and phenomenologists, he stresses Wells's premise that unless life seems meaningful, it is not worth the trouble. The point seems simplistic until Wilson ties it in with his emerging philosophy. Before Wilson's *new* existentialism one could glimpse only dimly the goal out there in the "noosphere." That goal already exists, however, in the mind-as-intention. But afraid of optimism, philosophers before Wilson had failed to identify Outsiderism as a symptom of an unrest which, when positively potentiated, will liberate men.

Wilson discusses what he labels "Romanticism" as first a symptom of that unrest and then as a partial breakthrough. Wilson concludes that Romanticism, symbolized by Lord Byron's Manfred who shakes his fist at God, ultimately failed when it dissolved pity and Faustian despair. The "second assault on the Bastille" of indifference by the *new* Romanticism (i.e., *old* existentialism) is exemplified, Wilson claims, by the works of Martin Heidegger, Karl Jaspers, and Gabriel Marcel, all of whom added a philosophical precision, which nevertheless did not ameliorate the old despair. Life remained meaningless; and the usual adjustments to despair — namely, endurance, resignation, or rebellion — failed to achieve satisfactory resolutions.

Wilson's *new* existentialism, which he begins definitely to reach for in this volume, redefines reality. It is based upon the conclusions of Edmund Husserl and Maurice Merleau-Ponty (as Wilson interprets them) that reality is something much more than, and much different from, the reality assumed by physics and originally underwritten by positivism. Wilson rejects the relatively dull reality proposed by science and docilely accepted by the layman. In place of such passiveness, Wilson proposes a new society which will work for the "heightening of creative vitality in all its members" (45). Wilson charges that all his predecessors have been inadequate to the task of designing such a society. Surveying the history of philosophy, Wilson sees only a muddle of despair and failure. Furthermore, literature has also reached a dead end, and music has developed parallel troubles. Philosophy, however, is allegedly in the worst trouble of all.

The confusion began with René Descartes and his "radical doubt." *Testing for truth* led inevitably to endorsing science and encouraging its dreadful child, behaviorism. Psychological behaviorists began to test the validity of traditional concepts such as the unconscious and the will. Radical doubt permeated laboratories and new vocabularies were developed. Operationism, for example, which tries to specify qualities as the quantities of what one has to *do* to get the effect of the quality, made it possible to *measure* what was formerly considered subjective rather than objective. Wilson, predictably, scorns attempts to *measure* certain aspects of living. Dismissing as itself meaningless the claim of logical positivism that anything that cannot be "reduced to logic" is meaningless, Wilson calls that philosophy "an emotional gesture of despair in the face of complexity" (66) — one similar to Marx's reduction of history to economics and Freud's reduction of religion to sexual needs. Wilson also compares the Cartesian fallacy, which assumes man's "I think" as central to philosophical concerns, with the Ptolemaic fallacy, which assumes the earth as central to the universe. In contrast, Wilson claims that complications vanish at "the centre of gravity of philosophy [which] should be the recognition of the 'I' behind the 'I think.' The starting point is still the 'I think,' the questioning intelligence. But instead of looking out at the universe from its armchair, it now needs two faces — one to look out; one to look inward towards the 'hidden I,' the transcendental ego" (69).

Wilson sees himself as the logical candidate, coming *after* Whitehead and Husserl as he does, to develop a *new* existentialism that he believes can be as factual and as logical as logical positivism was. Wilson would add to reality, however, other phenomena of human experience usually outlawed by his predecessors, Whitehead and Husserl. Whitehead had distinguished between "presentational immediacy" and "causal efficacy". The former, "presentational immediacy," is a kind of catchall for "thoughtless," more or less meaningless awareness; the latter, "causal efficacy," subsumes all stepped-up awareness in which the elements are bound into meaningful relationships. The Gestalt psychologists, of course, have always insisted that a person is innately capable of perceiving form and meaning and that humans intuitively make patterns out of the bits and pieces of experience. The behavioral psychologists, however, insist on differentiating the raw data of sensations — those responses to light, sound, odors, and other forms of energy which the organism reflexively makes — from those meaningful perceptions which the organism must *learn* to recognize. Wilson follows Whitehead and the Gestaltists in giving more credit to man's innate powers and less credit to environmental influences, that is, to experience. Furthermore, he credits man with the capacity to *willfully* control many of his perceptions. In a word, unlike behavioral scientists, he emphasizes intentionality. Also, he is interested in occultism, an area not quite respectable to most other philosophers.

In a quick survey of pertinent philosophers, Wilson separates the bad ones, who empty the human organism of all intentionality, from the good ones, who fill the organism with built-in perceptions and personal power to intensify those perceptions. Wilson makes a distinction between the *real* reality of philosophers who are not limited in their speculations by an experimental methodology and the *imputed* reality of logicians. He opts for that *real* experience which correlates with real reality against imputed experience. Wilson finds post-Cartesian philosophy guilty of failing to notice that it is possible to look at *real* reality in a *real* way — that is, experientially. He denounces the traditional, pre-Husserl kind of philosophy because it neglected meaning-perception. He accuses the narrow science of logical positivism of limiting its search for reality to peering through microscopes and telescopes. He rashly asserts that scientific method was never meant to be applied to philosophy, which he feels should be concerned with the nature both of the universe in general and of human life in particular.

Fixing conveniently upon Whitehead's term "prehension" as descriptive of the basic activity of consciousness, Wilson emphasizes man's capacity to intensify his prehending. Man prehends what and how much he wants to, Wilson claims. He cites some rather dusty evidence from famous psychological experiments with perceptions, such as the one in which an apparent Maltese cross is *really* a four-leaf clover, or an apparent four-leaf clover is *really* a Maltese cross, depending upon the intentionality of the perceiver. It thus follows, according to Wilson's own intentions, that the world as usually prehended by others is not the *real* world.

The so-called natural standpoint of physics, for example, has blinkered the bad philosophers who have been concerned only with polishing their systems: they have not *willed* to see what more there is to be seen than their disciplines have allowed. Instead, they have chosen to cut down on uncertainty and its greater number of degrees of freedom in order to benefit from the increased rigor of systematic observations. The rigorous scientist, for example, asks the only question he can answer: he asks *how* something comes about rather than *why* it happens. Husserl decided to set aside these ordinary prehensions in an attempt "to outwit the 'natural standpoint' by treating it as completely alien" (82). Husserl sought and presumably found evidence for the existence of intentionality. The importance to Wilson of Husserl's discovery is that he needs to establish intentionality in human behavior in order to defeat despair.

Wilson, who endorses so-called intentional evolution, believes that humans *tried* to be different from animals. Lower organisms must remain alerted to signals which indicate danger, food, and shelter or they do not survive. A human being, however, no longer needs to respond to everything "out there;" as a result, he has developed the capacity to be bored and indulges in luxurious inattentions which animals cannot afford. Wilson illustrates his point with an example of a man who is trying to protect himself from anxiety by resorting to boredom. "When a man yawns in a dentist's waiting room and says 'I am bored' he does not realize that his boredom — that seems the cheapest and most common thing in the world — has been purchased by millions of years of effort; as a commodity, it is more expensive than radium" (88). Regarding the world not perceivable by science as "primitive," Wilson endorses all attempts to discover that original life-world as good, as consciousness-expanding. Wilson implies that it takes a civilized mind to perceive properly the primitive! By the same token he rejects all philosophers who have stressed the importance of man's accepting life as a series of accidental events which he is powerless to alter and which therefore are said to be fated or contingent.

Wilson is impatient with the despair which comes from believing that man's life is contingent. In order to get rid of that despair, he is determined to cut down on the contingency. Accepting contingency, Wilson notes, can result in making life meaningless, or it can result in "proving" that Cartesianism is in error. The fact that Wilson's alternatives are not quite true alternatives underlines his urgency, for he is eagerly searching for subtle ways around or over the contingency-impasse. It is clear, however, why he must reject Sartre, Heidegger, and other philosophers who deny full intentionality to humans.

Wilson's "organising principle" in life and in evolution insists upon purposiveness in the evolutionary process. For example, he agrees with T. E. Hulme that evolution included "the gradual insertion of more and more freedom into matter" (120). Thus Wilson is sympathetic with Jean Lamarck's attempts to discredit mechanistic Darwinism. He sees himself as at least a neo-Darwinian, like Julian Huxley, who has tried to preserve religious values in a godless universe. All in all, Wilson grasps at and sometimes reaches anything that will reinforce his own conviction that man is a purposive being; and the most compelling evidence of this purposiveness for Wilson is clearly the unrest of his Outsider.

Now he can urge the Outsider to shuck off his despair by accepting his part in evolutionary intentionality. Distinguishing between the "Wells-Huxley position on evolution," which Wilson calls a "telenomy," and the phenomenological view, which he calls "evolutionary intentionality," and envisioning the emergence of what he calls a *consistent* "evolutionary humanism" (130), Wilson believes that he has moved *beyond the Outsider.*

He rests his case on the testimony of the awakened: "For those who have experienced it, the hour of the awakening of the passion for knowledge is the most memorable of the lifetime. It is the moment when it seems self-evident that man needs no religion of divine authority and commandments. Religion in that sense is a need of the animal, who needs it as a dog needs a master. The passion for knowledge replaces the need for faith, and purpose becomes an *internal drive*" (133 - 34).

Man is, therefore, the controlling agent not only of his personal consciousness but also possibly of the transcendent Consciousness. There are, however, certain problems which Wilson has not solved. For example, answering the *why* of a person's actions with a simple *because he willed it* only introduces another *why* about that willing. Behavioral science avoids such an infinite regress of *why's* by staying with the specifications of the *how* as the limit of useful knowledge. Be that as it may, asking for a significant change in man's mode of consciousness, Wilson calls upon phenomenologists, existentialist psychologists, and other concerned people to develop the means to that end. Anxious to "replace that sense of individual meaning, the feeling of having a direct telephone line to the universal purpose" which science took from mankind, Wilson calls upon those who support human *interior forces* "ultimately to establish the new evolutionary type foreshadowed by the 'outsiders' " (164).[12]

Citing *The Outsider,* as well as H. G. Wells's projections in *Star Begotten* and Howard Fast's fictions, Wilson finds overwhelming evidence of the imminent birth of man which is to be followed by an even more important event, the emergence of supermen. But Wilson is cautious; he admits that "there is no point in talking about the superman, because *man does not yet exist*" (167). Dead set against defeatism, a worthless legacy from the past, Wilson does not hesitate to predict as inevitable precisely that which he is exhorting man to do, just as Marx described his revolution as inevitable, and yet asked man to begin the new world. All reformers who claim inevitability for their vision of a better life are subject to the same logical fallacy — If it is going to happen anyway, why bother to urge men to act? Is inevitability, then, just another one of the many faces of contingency?

Colin Wilson is not so ingenuous as not to be aware of this sticky problem. He has, however, chosen to transcend it. He is justified in his own terms, for he has all along insisted upon the inadequacy of logical arguments to convey his messages and to divert others from error. As a matter of important fact, he has simultaneously been energetically projecting his vision in his fictions and in his fables. After the fashion of a prophet, he has occasionally paused in his sermons to say: "Let me tell you a story. Perhaps *that* will help you understand me. . . ."

By this time, most of the fun in attacking Wilson had dissipated. The young writer's persistence had given the lie to predictions that he would soon disappear from the scene. Accustomed to being called incompetent, Wilson must have been more pleased than disturbed to read that he had now become "stunningly incompetent."[13] Critics now admitted that Wilson, wrong as he might still be, was a man with a big vision; that, in fact, he was "engaged in boldly setting the whole intellectual world to rights."[14] Although Wilson's philosophical position was characterized as "upbeat" and "kitsch" by one excited Christian critic,[15] a more temperate verdict came from the anonymous reviewer in London, where perhaps Wilson still had a friend, who concluded that Wilson's "new book offers an argument which, if it is not quite adequately sustained, is yet almost consistently referred back to and sometimes carried forward and which is both tenable and heartening."[16]

In summary, by 1965 Wilson had extended his Outsider cycle into six volumes, had endured and survived both trivial and fair negative reactions to his work, and had steadily refined his message. Such refinement does not, however, necessarily improve the communication, especially if the putative receiver of the message is not adequate to receive in good faith the information that man *can* save himself if he becomes the driver of the intentional vehicle of his own salvation.

Colin Wilson is not, of course, the only would-be-savior who has decided to reject despair and anxiety as irreducible parts of the human condition. Other voices from other wildernesses have long been exhorting forlorn humanity to find itself, and sick humanity to heal itself. Over one hundred years ago Mary Baker Eddy, for example, tried to put Christianity on a working and *scientific* basis so that the faithful practitioners of "Christian Science" could heal not only themselves but others by "knowing the Truth" — namely, that man is made in the image and likeness of God and therefore cannot be sick or weak or impoverished. Such positive thinking eventually was secularized and detached from theological considerations, so that divine sanctions had nothing directly to do with a person's feeling better or working more efficiently or more creatively. Man was encouraged to heal himself by knowing himself.

Insight therapies, such as that underwritten by the American psychologist Carl Rogers, are most effective, however, only with intelligent patients not too sick to talk it out and not too dull to understand the treatment. Colin Wilson, also, makes his appeal to a limited group, those capable of willing themselves a new freedom. He is not an irresponsible messiah charismatically gathering multitudes of followers. He asks for hard-headed thinking about the problems he would have men solve.

CHAPTER 4

The Outsider as Novelist: I

COLIN Wilson considers his novels — which include special versions of psychological thrillers, spy stories, science fiction, nonfiction, and one of the first beat stories — as an integral part of his program to defeat defeatism. He believes that fiction is an appropriate vehicle for philosophical concerns. Early in his career he spelled out his commitment: "If I were to prescribe a rule that all future philosophers would have to obey it would be this: that no idea shall be expressed that cannot be expressed in terms of human beings in a novel — and perfectly ordinary human beings at that — not Peacockian brain-boxes. If an idea cannot be expressed in terms of people, it is a sure sign it is irrelevant to the real problems of life."[1] Even in his midway autobiography, he asserted that "the proper place for autobiography is fiction" *(Voyage,* 1).

As a matter of fact, none of Wilson's prose fiction has that kind of inevitability which awes literary critics, but it is honestly adequate to its purpose. Readers of novels are less reluctant to suspend disbelief, and they are willing to be persuaded by literary incantations as much as by ideas. Wilson knows what he is trying to do in his stories, and he has indicated his awareness of the technical problems involved in writing serious fiction.

Although Wilson is neither a Romantic nor a Naturalist, and although he eschews most avant-garde techniques, he has nevertheless endorsed "the Brechtian alienation effect," and claims that each of his fictions announces itself as such: "This is not reality, it is a novel, just as Brecht says: 'This is not reality but a play.' " Wilson has also characterized his novels as close to "parodies of novels, of particular genres."[2] There may be, of course, some rationalization in his theory, for conscious attempts to alienate readers by encouraging them not to *believe* in the story are sometimes indistinguishable from technical failures. This study of

Colin Wilson, however, tries to take his fiction as seriously as he does and thus largely accepts his texts as intentional creations rather than as contingent or accidental events. His failure to achieve verisimilitude in much of his fiction is really no failure at all if the effect of not being real was intended.

I Ritual in the Dark

The title of Wilson's first novel, *Ritual in the Dark* (1960), is significant. An attempt to invoke the dark mystery, Wilson claims for it an intricate and solemn genesis.[3] This ambitious work went through several major revisions before publication. Somewhat mysteriously, Wilson has claimed that his first novel is to *The Egyptian Book of the Dead* what Joyce's *Ulysses* is to the *Odyssey*. At least, it is clear that the novel is carefully structured to support its purposiveness. The authorial voice, never present as first person, is divided between several young Outsiders: Gerard Sorme, a writer; Austin Nunne, a dilettante and murderer; and Oliver Glasp, a painter. These youths are supplemented in the craftily designed patterns of the book by secondary characters securely interlocked with one another and with the main characters. The secondary characters include a German psychiatrist, a Scottish detective, and a wise old priest. All significances, however, are filtered through Gerard Sorme: the reader finally sees as Gerard sees, for ultimately only Gerard is a reliable witness.[4]

The novel begins simply with a once-upon-a-time opening, and the scene is London. Gerard Sorme, annoyed by the oppressiveness of the city, casually drops in to see an exhibit honoring Diaghilev and Nijinsky. There he meets a fellow named Austin Nunne, a man who superficially resembles the late Nijinsky and who confides to Gerard that he is the author of a "slim volume" about the mad dancer as well as a book about the ballet. Gerard, who is also working on a novel about Nijinsky, identifies Austin as a homosexual. Although he does not share his new friend's sexual predilections, he is attracted to him. Gerard and Austin soon begin to explore each other's psyches and minds in an accelerating friendship which takes them to bars and to their respective pads, of which Austin has several. As Gerard emerges as more and more complex, Austin appears less and less so; and there is little surprise when Austin is identified as a murderer. Both fascinated and repelled by Austin, Gerard also becomes interested in Austin's spinster aunt, Gertrude Quincy, a forty-year-old Jehovah's Witness, and later in Gertrude's niece, Caroline, a pretty young blonde. When Austin Nunne flies to Switzerland on one of his mysterious journeys, Gerard changes his own living quarters to avoid an entanglement with one of his old girl friends.

Without fussiness, Wilson brings together the people he wants to bring together in order to make his points. Thus, Gerard's new room sets the occasion for additional plot developments. One of Gerard's neighbors, a Frenchman by the name of Edmond Gallet, tells Gerard about the other strange tenants in the house. Carlotta, a German girl who works for the landlord, has a room in the basement; above Gerard lives an eccentric old man who plays records all night and sleeps during the day; two homosexuals occupy an apartment on the ground floor — and all of these neighbors eventually touch Gerard's life on several levels. He soon learns that the old man is suspected of committing the "Whitechapel murders." That night, after reading a book about murder left behind by the previous tenant and after being informed by Gallet that another girl has just been brutally killed in Whitechapel, he falls into fitful sleep only after fantasying a love scene with Austin's aunt.

Gerard is one of Wilson's most sensitive Outsiders; and, as such, he experiences "vastations" in which he doubts his own existence. He is also susceptible to fits of anger and deep depression, Once, when Gerard comes upon his upstairs neighbor who is quite naked, he is startled to discover the he feels an impulse to kill the old man. It is apparent that Gerard's indifference threshold is low; and Wilson is obviously preparing him for significant psychophilosophical perceptions.

When Austin calls Gerard from Switzerland and asks him to dispose of some female clothing in one of his two apartments, Gerard does not resist him despite his suspicions that Austin is criminally implicated; in fact, Gerard avidly searches for evidence that Austin is a sadistic murderer. After Gerard becomes sexually involved with Austin's Aunt Gertrude as well as with the luscious Caroline, he begins to apprehend more clearly the awesome potential which his encounter with the eccentric Austin has begun to liberate in himself.

On one of his errands to Austin's hideaway, Gerard discovers many books on pornography and sadism as well as four pornographic prints signed "O.G." and two morbid paintings signed "Oliver Glasp." His curiosity aroused, he decides to find the artist, whom he locates at work in a dismal studio apartment. A tall, red-haired, unkempt fellow, Glasp both attracts and repels Gerard. Like Austin and

Gerard, Glasp is an Outsider and also interested in murder. His great-aunt, he brags, was the last victim of Jack the Ripper. His mother once dined with the famous murderer Landru, in Paris, and his great-grandfather had known the so-called Banner Cross Murderer, Charley Peace.[5] Glasp identifies himself as "a conscious masochist" (160).

When Austin returns, he urges Gerard to leave England with him; but Gerard prefers London, where he feels he has been recovering a sense of purpose. After a drinking bout with Austin in which Gerard gets sick, Gerard has a dream in which Austin turns into Nijinsky. Soon thereafter, Gerard's temporary equilibrium is disturbed by the reports of a murder in Greenwich and of two more murders in Whitechapel.

A series of symposiumlike episodes follows in which Gerard's education is advanced. Glasp talks about sex and lust; and Gerard, Austin's counselor, Father Carruthers, and a German psychiatrist, Stein, discuss famous crimes. Stein explains *Lustmord* as "motiveless joy murder" (241). The priest suggests that "sex is the favorite human device for summoning the spirit" (243). When, however, Gerard later experiments with Gertrude, he experiences no such ecstasy. Soon thereafter Gerard deflowers Gertrude's niece, Caroline; and, because the act is painful for her and his own climax unbearably intense, he has a new insight: "Abruptly he knew it was not a cheat. What was happening now was realler than any of his thoughts about sex, more real than anything except pain: it was an intimation of the reason behind the tireless continuity of life" (255-56). Wilson's point is that in a successful sex act the partners both inflict and receive pain. Ideally, sexual intercourse is an imaginative, creative act in which the spectrum of feeling is extended through increased sensitivity to pain.

Gerard tries to justify as liberating acts the murders he is sure Austin has committed — the brutal stabbing of four female prostitutes within eleven months. Even murder is potentially creative when done by a superior person, for the act releases a sense of power. "Nothing matters but this power," Gerard argues. "No price is too high for it" (318). Anyway, he rationalizes, because Austin's victims had no reason to live, they lost only half lives: "And the killer himself was probably only half alive too. In that case, it was a case of quarter-murder. Futility murdering stupidity and uselessness. Nietzsche had said that a whole nation was a detour to create a dozen great men . . ."(322). In an effort to exorcise his disturbing empathy for Austin's crimes, Gerard confides in Austin's aunt; but her platitude-dominated comprehension is inadequate. She does agree, however, to take Gerard to Austin, who is hiding from the police. The subsequent scene between Austin and Gerard is a multileveled confrontation in which the tension is psychological rather than dramatic. There is no mystery, for Austin is clearly a murderer; and there is little probability of any more physical violence. One is concerned, if at all, only with Gerard's psychospiritual state and not with Austin; for the novelist has never promised dramatic denouements.

Gerard is fully aware of his affection for his killer-friend, and he recognizes that he is not really horrified. Austin's defense, as Gerard talks with him, is straight-forward self-justification. Of the motivation for his killing four women within one year, Austin says: "It's something in here. I feel sometimes that I could take an emetic and get rid of it all. It's like periodic malaria. But try to understand, Gerard. *It's not just a disease.* It's an excitement. It's a kind of inverted creative impulse. I feel as if I'm serving something greater than myself. It's . . . it's like a need . . . to build" (394). Such desperate sincerity momentarily persuades Gerard: "He felt a curious acceptance of Austin Nunne; it was no more strange that Nunne should be a murderer than that he should be a homosexual" (396). Inevitably, Gerard counters with a confession of his own. "I belong among the Enemies," he tells Austin: "certain men whose business is to keep the world in a turmoil — the Napoleons, Hitlers, Genghis Khans" (398).

Before the police terminate the conversation by arresting Austin, Gerard and his friend have experienced their moment of truth — a communion between Outsiders. Although Gerard at first bluntly refuses to testify against his friend, Professor Stein urges him to reconsider and at least go to the morgue to view the mutilated body of Austin's latest victim, another female prostitute. Gerard agrees and is surprised to find that his sympathy is not aroused by the corpse. But, when he looks at another body near by, that of a woman burned to death, he is deeply moved. The corpse to which Gerard is supposed to react is too disfigured to seem human: it is an *it,* not a *woman.* Because the second corpse — although badly burned — is still identifiable as an attractive woman, Gerard responds. Killing now signifies to him: "Suddenly I realized what it meant — death by violence. It's a complete negation of all our impulses. It means we've got no future. And it's not just a question of my future — it's the future of the human race" (437).

Gerard no longer sees Austin as a valiant rebel who is trying to throw off his Outsiderism through the imaginative use of sex, sadism, and killing. He suddenly realizes Austin is truly insane rather than "supersane." In the end, Austin's aunt, at Gerard's urging, promises to persuade Austin's wealthy family to "put him away," thereby preventing him from doing any more violence, since the police have insufficient evidence to indict the killer. As this solution indicates, Wilson is not interested in murder-will-out justice. For the philosopher who is using the novel to promote ideas, the narrative climax occurs when Gerard perceives the contradiction between his compassionate identification with a murderer and his own positive social goals. Because of Austin Nunne's insanity, his creative impulses misfired; but creativity is always risky.

Wilson addresses himself in this first novel to an important concern, namely, the coordinates of that line which separates man and beast; but, whether he succeeded or not, his objective was seriously questioned. The sombre jacket of the first edition of *Ritual in the Dark* quotes "high praise" from the *London Sunday Express:* "Not since Dickens has a British fiction-writer dealt with murder in a book of such size and seriousness." Sympathetic American critics made allowances for the fact that the work was a first novel. One reviewer called it "extraordinary" although "not faultless, for Sorme, explaining his developing theories to a succession of people, is sometimes repetitious. There is an inordinate amount of talking about, negotiating for and drinking tea, which may well be true to life, but if so, constitutes excessive naturalism."[6] Another reviewer admired the "author's own intellectual passion and moral earnestness."[7]

Ritual in the Dark is marked by the usual faults of a first novel: insistence on its own significance and subordination of craft. The novel is equally marked, however, by the virtues of a first work: fresh material and new perspectives on that material, and the kind of youthfulness that was called "utterly alive and engrossing."[8] Although it was ungracious of one reviewer to assert that the "illusion Author Wilson may have to kill is that he is a born novelist,"[9] Wilson had good reason not to despair so soon in his career. The work is given prominence in this study because it typifies Wilson's use of fiction to promote his ideas. The negative verdict of a reviewer who called the novel "one of the worst pieces of fiction ever written" was fairly qualified when the critic added that "at the same time, since it is not cluttered with chunks from other people's books, it has the naive charm of direct revelation."[10] What more could young Wilson hope for than to be nominated as a prophet!

II Adrift in Soho

Wilson's second novel, *Adrift in Soho* (1961), is relatively light in mood. Partly autobiographical and partly adapted from a friend's manuscript, its effect is always personalized, for it is a first-person narrative.[11] Some of the material had been used by Wilson in an unsuccessful play, *The Metal Flower Blossom;* and, although the novel received some thoughtful reviews, it remains an odd item in the Wilson canon. Although Wilson reports in *Voyage to a Beginning* that his publisher, Gollancz, said it had the "*perpetuum mobile* quality of a Viennese waltz" (254), the "beat" is more folk-rock than Austrian and is definitely akin in content to Jack Kerouac's romantic fables. Wilson, however, wears his beatific vision with a difference; for, in his solemnly escalating search for truth, he rejects *la vie bohème* because he finds the Soho rebels superficial.

The narrator, a young man named Harry, has trouble readjusting to his old life in the Midlands after having been abruptly discharged from the Royal Air Force. He decides to become a writer, but after two weeks of trying to write six hours a day in a dreary local library while paying five pounds a week board at home, Harry goes to work as a laborer. For a few days he is stimulated by manual labor; but, quickly falling into a depression, he breaks with home and moves to London where he finds a bed at a youth hostel in Great Ormond Street. Harry's first evening excursion takes him all around Soho. Disappointed because the local characters look more like "spivs and racing touts" (19) than writers and actors, Harry begins to suspect he will not find the kind of freedom he is looking for. He senses hostility: "The whole city was a part of the great unconscious conspiracy of matter to make you feel nonexistent" (20).

After renting a small, overpriced room in an imposing house in Earl's Court, he is evicted the very next morning for sharing his room with a new-found friend, an unemployed young actor improbably named Charles Compton Street, and with Charles's girlfriend of the evening. Harry also falls in with a New Zealand girl, Doreen. Thanks to his new friends, who know how to cope, Harry adjusts to the ways of Soho within forty-eight hours after his arrival. He also acquires an admission card for the British Museum Reading

Room and soon learns how to pass time inexpensively by loitering in cafes and shops, bumming meals off tourists, and sleeping on late suburban trains. When Doreen is evicted from her living quarters because Harry has spent the night with her, he finds a place for the girl in a Notting Hill pad which includes, ad lib, beds and bedmates as well as food and marijuana.

Harry has now met a sampling of genuine Soho characters. However, he soon wearies of Charles's evasions and is cheated on a book deal by another new friend, the so-called Count Robert de Bruyn. He meets and likes Marty Roberts, reputed to be one of the best chess players in Europe, and "Ironfoot Jack," the "uncrowned king of the bohemians," from whom he buys a small pair of scissors; Harry comments at the time that he has always had a "weakness for cutting instruments, which may be explained by a family rumor that Jack the Ripper was a distant relative" (66).

A significant moment occurs when Harry is moved by a picture of two Egyptian statues in the window of a bookshop in Tottenham Court Road. He understands instantaneously why he despises London. "The life people lived in this city," he tells himself, "was designed to interpose between man and that image of perfection" (75). Attracted to the easy life but simultaneously repulsed by the waste of talent and energy in Soho, he realizes that most of his new friends are shiftless rather than really free. For example, Vera merely drifts from one bed to another. Hoffman, a solvent middle-aged journalist whom the younger rebels exploit, is addicted to lighting grate fires with gasoline. Tilly and Desmond have become the official shoplifters for the casual community. Robby Dysart, "England's greatest poet after Dylan Thomas," seems completely disorganized (99). Sir Reginald Propter, part-time member of the group and editor of a Hollywood magazine for Vedantists, simply talks and talks and talks.

In the Notting Hill house, Harry at first shares Doreen's bed although he feels no sexual urgency. Pleasantly "aroused" by the presence of Doreen, he is however, more interested in his awareness "of a rhythm of living that would parallel the vibration of the powerhouse" (124) than in sex. Thus, instead of seducing Doreen, Harry contemplates the significance of his not doing so. In bed, the proximity of the desirable woman sparks his imagination more than his lust; and, in this heightened mood, Harry realizes that the "bohemian life" may truly be a bore.

Harry's progress through Soho becomes a kind of parable. He

notes that only Ricky Prelati, the host-manager of the house on Notting Hill, is unlike Oswald Blichstein, a self-styled Satanist, and Blichstein's willowy companion, Eric Primrose, in that he is sufficiently disciplined to turn the chaos around him into some meaning. Meanwhile, the conversations in the house become heavier and heavier with Huxleyean intellectualism. After Harry smokes his first marijuana cigarette, he tries to make love to the willing Vera, but his weak stomach and his vision of the absurdity of the sex act intervene. Again that night he sleeps with Doreen without making love to her either.

In the second part of the novel Harry explains more about Doreen and himself, emphasizing the fact that they continue to sleep together without making love. Unsurprisingly, he finally finds a bed for himself in a washroom abandoned by an unwashed Welshman, an eccentric who cultivates malodorousness in order to make people hate him so that he in turn may never be betrayed by friendship. Impressed, Harry understands momentarily that such a rejection of convention can be made in the name of love for the essence of humanity — for what people could really be.

The novel ends with a big party in celebration of the fact that Ricky's paintings have been discussed on television by Sir Reginald Propter. The ensuing publicity, however, annoys Ricky, who wants to go on working in his own way at his own speed, never doubting meanwhile his own genius and his own ultimate success. Harry is left contemplating the difference between Ricky's self-assurance and his own tentativeness. A true Outsider, Ricky may be the only one among all the rebels to elevate the Soho ways into a Way of Life. Presumably Harry, too, is now ready to chart his own course: he is no longer adrift in Soho.

The significance of this unpretentious novel in Wilson's canon, according to Wilson's American admirer, R. H. W. Dillard, is that it develops "the moral understanding a step further, pressing acceptance toward affirmation."[12] The novel was also praised for reflecting "the amoral social attitudes of a people without a past or a future," although it "opens no new literary panoramas."[13] More ingenuous than Kerouac's impressions of a parallel generation in America, *Adrift in Soho* was decried as "nouveau beat" in that Wilson's "crowd" was "apparently not hip enough to know marijuana from hashish."[14] Another critic decided the novel was for Wilson "a large step backward. Once again his adolescent notions of what are the Problems of Life are worked over with a humorless and autobiographical jauntiness, but there is less and less nourishment."[15] The fairest judgments on the book, however, stress ideas just as Wilson intended. A reader's needs as well as his experience determine a large part of his response to Wilson's novels, which are indisputable as far as taste goes. Didactic fiction is generically distasteful to some readers. Others find stories a waste of time unless they teach or inform in some clear way. Wilson's fiction is openly didactic. His characters are manipulated, their actions are choreographed for meaningful effects. Nothing is abstractedly artistic or designed for its own sake. Thus the American reviewer who praised *Adrift in Soho* as revealing the fact that its author "has an interesting mind" while asserting that "it is probably not a mind that will ever find its best expression in fiction,"[16] hit both targets accurately. The ability to ascertain the intelligence and good faith of Wilson's ideas from the novel testifies to the success of Wilson's use of the genre. Although the book is dated in content and provincial in setting, the message is durable. By avoiding slickness, intentionally, and missing greatness, perhaps less intentionally, the writer has kept faith with his reader.

III The Violent World of Hugh Greene

In 1963 Wilson published two more works of fiction: *The Violent World of Hugh Greene* and *The Sex Diary of Gerard Sorme.* Although the former was at first misread as a psychological thriller and consequently judged as lacking in thrills and the latter was indicted as pornography, both works are in fact serious projections of the author's convictions at the time and are designed to promote increased awareness in the reader and stimulate increased concern for the need for educational reforms and more open discussion of crime and sex.

The Violent World of Hugh Greene[17] is a slow-paced story told in the first person by a narrator who often stops to philosophize about the significance of his education and other experiences. In the tradition of the *Bildungsroman,* the work is concerned with identifying the most significant variables in the hero's growth and in fixing the sources of his mature convictions as well as strange habits. Like his creator, Hugh Greene emerges as a prodigy who was largely self-taught and extraordinarily eager for knowledge from an early age.

Encouraged by his father and two eccentric uncles, Nick and Sam, Hugh begins as a child to question the value of ordinary experience as an index to knowledge. The rites of his passage from "The Outer

Dark" to "The Inner Dark" (subtitles for the two parts of the novel) include the rigorous testing of the significance of both normal and criminal behavior. Minor brushes with schoolboy violence teach young Hugh the absurdity of abstract morality; but, although he feels the urge to meet violence with violence, he also feels a revulsion against violence. The conflict is obviously symptomatic of deeper problems.

At the age of eleven, Hugh witnesses a performance by a broken-down hypnotist, "The Great Kaspar." Although Kaspar does not succeed in hypnotizing him, Hugh comes away from the performance with respect for the power of hypnotism. Soon thereafter his fear of bullies is exorcised in a gang fight which ends in a victory for Hugh's side, and he feels the taste of triumph. As he matures Hugh continues to explore the importance of power based on a personal vitality. While still impressionable he discovers a strange book entitled *Old Truths with New Names,* which promotes the theory that wasters and drifters are sometimes endowed with a superabundance of energizers. He looks up the author, Jeremy Wolfe, and together they search out the limits of various esoterica, including supernatural phenomena. As his friendship with Jeremy opens new vistas to Hugh, he decides not to go to Cambridge: "Where before there had only been Newton and Gauss and Einstein, there was now the music of Delius, the dialogues of Plato, the novels of Tolstoy" (98).

The sixteen-year-old Hugh takes a job as a clerk in the office of the electricity board, but he is soon bored with the clerical routines. When, however, he meets Jeremy's "military type" cousin, Monty, and Monty's girl, Patricia, Hugh's lifespace expands; and he resumes his explorations into human relationships. Monty and Hugh get into a scrape with a couple of tough characters, but the toughs are no match for Monty. Pondering the contrast between Jeremy, a pacifist, and Monty, a warrior, Hugh concludes that both types are wrong; the cult of violence and that of antiviolence are both dead ends. Finally, he finds Jeremy and Monty absurd in that they are both unpotentiated.

One evening Hugh witnesses a violent scene in which a group of leather-coated teddy boys attack a youth and leave him sprawled on the sidewalk. Hugh identifies with the victim; and, as a result, he gradually begins to plan revenge. Moving toward the existential meaning of violence as distinguished from verbal abstractions, he joins a "revolver-club" and hopes to arrange a provocative encounter with the gang of toughs.

Meanwhile, when Monty confides in Hugh that he has lost Patricia as his mistress, Hugh pursues the girl; but he is unexpectedly repelled by her overeagerness to make love. She is no challenge to him. He prefers long walks alone as he searches the stars for meaning, and he dreams of moving the static, of breaking-through: "One god, one god-like human being, would change the course of history by showing men how to behave . . ." (135). He also eventually consummates his affair with Patricia, although he is still not excited sexually by her. At the gun club, after a few rounds of shooting, Hugh realizes that shooting is more real than anything else: "Ten minutes of good shooting can produce a feeling of health as complete as a moorland walk in a high wind" (148).

The novelist is now building toward the crisis — Hugh's fall to existence. When Monty's friend, Nigel, admits that he would enjoy beating a girl at least once a week, Hugh is not shocked. Nigel, a subsidiary character in the novel, resembles Austin Nunne in *Ritual*, but he lacks Austin's capacity to kill.

To Patricia's proposal of marriage, Hugh counters the insincere objection that he is only seventeen years old. The truth is that, after satisfying his curiosity about Patricia, he finds her tedious. For relief from the banalities of normalcy he begins to become involved with "real" criminal types such as Jed, to whom he is introduced by one of Monty's friends, a weird fellow who later is revealed to be Kaspar, the hypnotist of the episode in Hugh's childhood. Through Kaspar, Hugh also meets Dime, a pimp. The cast of characters for the decisive final episodes is now assembled: a small-time criminal, a broken-down hypnotist, a sex maniac, a repulsive pimp, a sexual athlete, a neurotic intellectual, a nymphomaniac, and an assortment of detectives and gun-club associates plus an ever-ready gang of teddy boys, one of whom is destined to be Hugh's victim.

As Hugh quickly brings the account of his life up to date, he reveals that he is presently thirty-two years old. The narrator all along has been commenting in terms of his mature perspective about past events. At seventeen, Hugh was vulnerable to the logic of absurdity; but, at thirty-two, his vulnerability has dwindled. He remembers that at seventeen, as he was loading his pistol preparatory to provoking the critical incident with the toughs which would justify his shooting one of them, it seemed to him that he "was about to strike a blow" against absurdity. From his mature perspective, he admits that he cannot explain the feeling: "I can see that I might just as well have felt that I was only increasing the absurdity" (183).

The critical incident is not dramatically projected. Instead, it partakes of all the equivocations of time-past remembered in the present. When confronted by the hostile gang in the backyard setup, the young Hugh bungles the act: he trips over an empty oil drum and drops his briefcase containing his two guns. A member of the gang finds one of the guns but does not suspect that there is a second weapon in the briefcase, which Hugh is able to retrieve in time to shoot at one of the youths after the teddy boy with the first gun has tried ineffectually to shoot him. Actually, Hugh fires two shots, the second one of which hits a lad who begins to moan that he has been killed. Hastily gathering together his case and his two guns, the second of which has finally been dropped by the wounded youth, Hugh retreats. The significance of the moment is its relative insignificance: the moment of which Hugh has dreamed as obliterating absurdity and giving his life meaning by liberating the imagination has fallen flat. The incident proves to be irrelevant.

After the shooting, although Hugh is depressed, he shrewdly sees that the next step in his education is concerned with the meaning of irrelevance. Nothing is *merely* irrelevant; it must be irrelevant *to* something. More interested in the philosophical implications of his position than in the danger of revengeful action by the gang or of detection by the police, Hugh broods much in the days that follow. He rejects suicide as pointless if life is meaningless. The papers, moreover, carry no mention of the shooting incident. Thus Hugh is disconcerted, for he begins to doubt even the reality of his plot against absurdity. The papers, however, do play up a recent sex crime, the strangling of a girl. Called to the police station, Hugh is surprised that he is questioned not about the shooting but about the identity of Jed, the sex maniac and the suspected strangler of the girl. Hugh refuses to identify Jed in a lineup procedure, although he clearly recognizes him. He soon discovers that Kaspar knows that Hugh shot a fellow, and Kaspar supposes that Hugh's failure to identify Jed is a bid for protection in exchange for identifying Jed. The jejune plot beings to close in, but there are really no further surprises and only one more unimportant killing, when Dime, for ill-defined reasons, murders Jed. What there is of suspense remains psychological and philosophical.

At this time Hugh has a "vastation" in which he confronts the "last level of meaninglessness" (216). "If all men are futile," he asks himself, "why had I been given a perception of the futility?" Evidently there is some other criterion by which degrees of futility are measurable, "some intuitive idea of health" (217). Hugh realizes that he has been superimposing his own sense of futility onto a neutral reality.

An unpleasant brush with the repulsive Dime makes it clear that Hugh is now considered an accessory to the strangling of the girl because of his refusal to identify Jed in the police lineup. Dime also reveals his knowledge of Hugh's attack on the ruffians. The assumption made by the *real* criminals is that Hugh will protect them as long as they protect him. Determined to find out what happened to his teddy-boy victim, Hugh learns through a friend of Patricia that the boy was not seriously hurt. Hugh now understands that there will be no attempt by the police to find him; nevertheless, the philosophical implications of his act still enchain him.

When Jed confesses to Hugh that he is the sex-killer, Hugh devises a rationale for Jed's crimes that equates Jed's "powers of concentration, of single-mindedness" with those which "a Newton might envy" (241). By concentrating, Jed was able to reduce women to objects. Although Jed's murder was an antisocial act, it was also highly imaginative.

From his attic hideaway Uncle Sam outlines for Hugh three possible resolutions of Hugh's uncertainty: suicide, action, or withdrawal. Trying to follow Sam's advice that he first define the "real problems," Hugh is surprised on the way home by a "bubble of happiness" (249). He feels with "a blaze of certainty" that "fate" is now on his side (253). As he ponders this evidence of his capacity for "inexplicable changes from exhaustion to rising vitality," he realizes that he is now dealing with "real problems" (253).

When shortly thereafter Hugh learns of the murder of Jed by Dime, Hugh's mood shifts first into ecstatic dizziness, then into depression, and finally into philosophical resignation. He relinquishes Patricia to a rich young man. After he himself inherits twenty thousand pounds from Uncle Sam, he uses his leisure time to continue his education in the British Museum Reading Room. Like his creator, in three months he reads "straight through" Berkeley, Hume, Kant, Hegel, and William James; and he also explores latter-day phenomenologists and psychologists. After discovering Husserl, he begins to define his own objectives: "to ask how far human prejudices and preconceptions have managed to creep into our 'objective' scientific knowledge" (265). He then decides to write a series of works which he is determined will be highly significant. Presumably, like Wilson himself, he will eventually found a new philosophy.

Critical opinion of the novel, as usual, was both negative and positive, often characteristically polarized in the same sentence. One reviewer said that the work "draws too crudely from newspapers and case histories, it's very pretentious and tails off feebly, but it's often stimulating!"[18] Praised as "intriguing" for superficial reasons, such as the mysterious aspects of the plot, and faulted as "irritating" for equally superficial reasons, such as its failure to sustain suspense in the reader, the work remains a kind of deliberate failure at the level at which Wilson intended it to be: a demonstration of just how subtly violent emotions are related to man's quest for the meaning of his own life as well as the bigger meaning of life. At the end of the novel, referring to his friend Jeremy, who has finally achieved peace with himself and "a certain local success," Hugh comments on the contrast between the mature Jeremy and the young "Proustian hermit" he had once known, noting the apparent contradictions in his friend's behavior. The last sentence in the book calls attention to Wilson's purpose in writing the novel. It suggests a justification for a philosopher's telling stories as well as trying to put together a systematic philosophy. He concludes, as if with a sigh, that "the contradictions of the bundle of responses called a human being can never be resolved as simply as the contradictions of philosophy" (272). If indeed Wilson intended to show how difficult living is compared to speculating about it, the mission of this novel succeeds to the extent that the violent world experienced by Hugh was finally only partly understood even by Wilson himself!

IV The Sex Diary of Gerard Sorme

Wilson's next experiment in fiction, *The Sex Diary of Gerard Sorme* (1963),[19] purports to be the intimate confession of the central character from *Ritual in the Dark*. It explicates certain obscurities in the earlier novel before it moves on to new material. The usual paraphernalia of the diary-genre are included, such as prefatory and appended notes claiming authenticity for the writings, culminating in a pious hope that readers "will see that the intentions were anything but pornographic — that, in fact, the book owes more to Gabriel Marcel's *Metaphysical Journal* than to Frank Harris" (viii). Wilson believed that in this work he was in fact making "a frontal attack on reality . . ."[20]

References in the early pages of the diary to Austin Nunne, Oliver Glasp, and other characters from *Ritual in the Dark* firmly link the work with the earlier novel. *The Sex Diary*, however, moves on to its own thesis, which is an emphatic demonstration of how sex and crime stimulate the imagination, and of how the stimulated imagination can in turn make a god out of a man. Insisting that his knowledge comes from his capacity to identify with violent behavior of all kinds, Gerard defends Austin more precisely in this novel than he did in *Ritual in the Dark*. In the earlier novel, Gerard had finally rejected Austin as insane; but he now insists "that Austin was dimly, vaguely trying to follow his own deepest nature to some unheard-of form of self-expression" (9). Identifying the "sexual force" as "the nearest thing to magic — to the supernatural — that human beings ever experience" (10), the diarist justifies the intensity of his own sex drive. He then proceeds to illustrate his sexuality so vividly that the novel had to be cleared in court before it could be sold in England — after which, of course, it sold fairly well.

Gerard describes in detail his seduction of Carlotta, a maid, to illustrate his "theory" that, "when a man and woman get into bed together, they imagine they are going to titillate one another; *there is no one else*, just the two of them. But this isn't ture. *There is a third*. In the very act of sex, they are performing an incantation that arouses the sex god, whose business is to drive the world in the direction of evolution" (40). Gerard tries to explain the how and the why of his sexual technique: "My method of attack is the same as that of Nietzsche, Kierkegaard, Wells: fragmentary, yet this is necessary. I make short, violent attacks on the faceless reality in an attempt to take it by storm, driven wholly by an intuition, not by reason. And sex is the ideal driving force for my pneumatic drill" (42 - 43).

Gerard's removal to new living quarters becomes the occasion for introducing a set of characters not found in *Ritual in the Dark*. Gerard's new neighbor, Kirsten, is a composer; and he claims to have learned how to live without compromising. Gerard agrees to write a libretto for him based upon the life of a seventeenth-century practitioner of black magic and sex orgies who fascinates Gerard. But the working out of the plotted complications begins in earnest when Gerard meets Caradoc Cunningham, an occultist and sexual athlete, at an exhibition of Oliver Glasp's painting. Cunningham, who is convinced that he is "loved by the gods" (101), claims to know the identity of Jack the Ripper as well as the identity of the "Whitechapel murderer" (Austin Nunne in *Ritual in the Dark*). Meanwhile, Gerard adds Kirsten's attractive wife, Diana, to his list of sex partners. After making love to her eight times in one night, he decides that "sex depends entirely upon the idea of the *violation of identity*" (115).

Carlotta now reports that Cunningham magically comes to her at night through a locked door to make love to her. Gerard at first grants Cunningham the power to make Carlotta *believe* this but not the power to materialize himself on the other side of a locked door. By the end of November, Gerard notes in his diary: "Things get crazier" (175). Cunningham begins to practice his black magic openly; and, when he uses Carlotta's body as an altar, Gerard feels exalted rather than disgusted.

Cunningham proposes a series of experiments to prove to Gerard that the sexual orgasm can be prolonged excessively. In the final scene Carlotta once again plays the central role but this time Cunningham adds such touches as magic pentagrams and a special brown powder, which turns out to be mostly Spanish fly. As the "mass" gets underway, evil spirits seem to enter the room; and Gerard faints. The denouement, which includes a police raid, results in Gerard's swearing off black magic for life and in the disappearance of Cunningham, although an "Author's Note" appended to the diary reports Cunningham's reappearance in Los Angeles as the founder of a new religion.

Critical reception of *The Sex Diary* followed the usual pattern of ambivalence, vituperation, and adulation. One critic hazarded a guess that "Colin Wilson himself is a spoof and that Kingsley Amis, Malcolm Muggeridge, and Peter Ustinov go away together on occasional weekends and compose a Colin Wilson book."[21] Another critic praised the novelist for his "honesty and vitality."[22] A few years later Wilson himself admitted that he viewed *The Sex Diary* as "a volume of tongue-in-cheek pornography and diabolism . . . which embodies, in fictional form, the ideas expounded in my phenomenological study, *Origins of the Sexual Impulse*."[23]

It is, of course, the better part of self-defense to plead "tongue-in-cheek" intentions after a work fails to be taken seriously. Fiction that distorts reality in the direction of making it seem worse than it is, as in satire, or that says the opposite of what it means, as in irony, always runs the risk of being misunderstood by literal-minded readers. It takes nimbleness as well as a firm grasp on reality to enjoy distorted representations of that reality. Colin Wilson does not play games comfortably. Thus his fiction, no matter how deliberately he may try to make it light or sardonic, usually comes out solemnly didactic. *The Sex Diary*, because of the subject matter, certainly seems to exaggerate reality, as pornography, by definition, is meant to do; but one comes away from the book, if he has read it in good faith, convinced that it is not pornography. One believes that Wilson did intend to tell the truth about sex intelligently and accurately.

By 1963 it was apparent that Wilson's fiction and nonfiction were complementary works that reinforced one another ideologically. By that time, five volumes of the Outsider cycle had, in accelerating enthusiasm, refined and elaborated his concern with outsiderism and possible remedies for mankind's malaise. Two major novels of the period, *Ritual in the Dark* and *The Violent World of Hugh Greene*, dramatize that malaise, with emphasis on the degenerate and criminal ways in which men have tried to adjust to life-forces they could feel but not creatively utilize. The essays in the Outsider cycle document the message of the novels: the contemporary human predicament in which man's knowledge has not yet been translated into wisdom.

If a book is an event between the reader and the writer, as behavioral psychologists propose, it is significant that both the reader and the writer are variables, whereas the text is the only constant. The text remains coldly objective until it is "read." Wilson's evangelical motives necessitate his trying to move the reader in all ways possible, and thus he uses different genres. Novels for him are means to the same end as that which his expository writing hopes to reach: a change in the reader as a response to the writer. Wilson's writings by 1963 show clearly how much he believes in the subjective aspect of the writing-reading experience. His novels are experiments in altering the reader's behavior. They are in a real sense variations on the themes of the essays in that they are also devices to catch the conscience of the reader.

CHAPTER 5

The Outsider as Novelist: II

As Colin Wilson's novels become more frankly didactic, they are also more skillfully written and thus more persuasive in their own terms. The logic of fiction can be as rigorous as the logic of science, but so-called science fiction achieves, at best, only a precarious credibility. For Wilson, fantasy is highly useful as a relatively unblinkered kind of storytelling, for he writes neither to delight nor to solace. He packs his parables with his own experiences and speculations. Since Wilson has a difficult message to communicate he needs all the help he can get in the way of supportive mysteries and heuristic fantasies.

I Necessary Doubt

Wilson's fifth novel, *Necessary Doubt* (1964),[1] takes its title from Paul Tillich's theology; and the main character, Professor Karl Zweig, is an "existential theologian." In this philosophical treatise which is lightly disguised as a novel, Zweig carries the burden of Tillichian concerns about the nature of God and man. A refugee early in the 1930s from Nazi Germany, Zweig has experienced both despair and hope intensely. To him, Wilson gives many of the arguments for a Christian revival, including the doubts which reinforce those arguments. According to Zweig, "man's capacity to doubt is his greatest dignity, and . . . even a saint should never discard his ability to doubt" (23).

The plot revolves around a "manhunt" for Gustav Neumann, the son of a famous surgeon whose unexpected suicide has aroused suspicions. The hunt begins on Christmas Eve in London when Zweig thinks he sees Gustav get into a taxi with an aged companion, but Zweig's awareness immediately transmutes the work from a cops-and-robbers chase to the pursuit of meaning. Zweig, who emotionally can identify with the hunted, is painfully aware of his responsibility. As Gustav's former teacher, as a close friend of the family, and as a social and sentient being, Zweig finds no solace in simple categories and tired truisms. Intent as he is on being in good faith, he quickly reaches the end of traditional paradigms. Paradoxically, the hunted in this novel carries less guilt than the hunter.

Zweig is a convincing projection. Wilson himself grew up believing fervently that someday, somehow, he would find all the answers or at least rewrite the questions so that they could be answered. But existence precedes essence. The elderly Zweig is no enthusiast sleeping out on Hampstead Heath and haunting the British Museum to read and dream. His many books are solid. Although his ideas have frequently been disagreed with, his work as a whole has been respected. He is what Germans call *ein Mensch*. He is also mature enough to know his weaknesses. His age relieves him from anxiety at not having much sexual passion while it excuses his reluctance to act. As a true philosopher, however, Zweig is a great man *manqué*. The irony soon surfaces: intellect is not sufficient. Zweig was a *mere* philosopher: Gustav, in contrast, had "returned to the body" (301).

As Zweig reassembles his memories of the Gustav he used to know and teach, he becomes increasingly troubled by the logic of circumstantial evidence which begins to identify Gustav as a criminal and by the psychologic which at the same time indicates that Gustav could not be a real criminal. Ultimately it is the definition of "criminal" which resolves the apparent contradiction. The young Gustav himself had theorized that the world had not yet produced a really great criminal, for even Hitler had been a fool. Gustav had early confided in his friend-teacher his ambition to become a master criminal, "the first criminal in the history of the human race who is not just an underprivileged victim" (28). Now Zweig rationalizes his pursuit of Gustav as a friendly gesture, believing most of the time that his young friend could not *really* be a murderer. Zweig does admit, however, that the affair "makes a good story. In the hands of a writer of detective stories it could be fascinating" (39). This point is important, for Wilson is deliberately discounting detective stories while busily writing one, hoping, in this way, to alert the reader to the trickery in order to create a feeling of distance between reader and book and thus encourage the reader to think more for himself.

In the Dostoevskian tradition, Zweig has several dreams. In one of them, he is playing chess with Gustav when suddenly he and Gustav turn into chessmen on a huge board while, at the same time, Zweig remains looking down on the board. It is apparent that Zweig is having trouble distinguishing between dreams and memories on the one hand and so-called reality on the other. Excitedly he speculates about the possibility of a murderer remaining "outside his own act." He asks himself: "Wouldn't this be the final expression of free will — to kill without involvement?" (61).

Eventually Zweig is joined in the hunt for Gustav by two friends, an eccentric mystic and a stereotyped detective. Evidence points to Gustav's present situation as a secretary-companion to Sir Timothy Ferguson, an aged rich man who resembles Gustav's other alleged victims, as a threat to his patron's life. After Gustav is located at Sir Timothy's secluded cottage, a series of confrontations between Zweig and Gustav promote the philosophical implications of the novel. While the police are kept at bay, as they are in the climax scenes in Wilson's *Ritual in the Dark* and *The Glass Cage*, Gustav explains his actions to his old teacher.

Gustav reminds Zweig that Gustav's father, before he committed suicide, had been obsessed with the idea that everyone wastes his life. Convinced that his father had been right, Gustav concentrated on the problem of futility. He worked alone, because by that time Zweig had deserted him for Christianity. As part of the explanation, Zweig swallows a pill given to him by Gustav; and the effect of the pill on Zweig dramatizes Gustav's claim that he has found an antidote to defeatism. Believing that mankind has been unnecessarily complacent, Gustav has been testing the reactions of various chemicals on man's awareness; and Gustav's pill, which contains the substance neuromysin, almost immediately makes Zweig feel more energetic and liberated. This drug, which has become Gustav's secret weapon, is used with his skill as a hypnotist to help old and sick people maximize energy and minimize waste until they, *of their own free wills*, decide to commit suicide. Gustav long ago reached an important conclusion: "Everything is inside us; all we have to do is pull the switch" (269). Gustav's drug, however, is not yet a universal panacea. In a man who is undisciplined or in a neurotic, neuromysin would produce undesirable reactions and release brakes that should not be released lest the stimulated weakling harm others.

Wilson introduces other by-now familiar subtleties into his story by ordering degrees of doubt along a distribution ranging from total skepticism to total faith. Gustav and Zweig discuss Gustav's so-called criminal career, which Gustav claims benefited his victim-friends immeasurably. In order to finance his researches Gustav had accepted unusual commissions, such as the one in which he guaranteed to relieve a dying man of pain for as long as possible. Predictably, the man eventually chose suicide as the most effective and certainly the most permanent solution. Technically, Gustav was guilty of at least manslaughter in these cases; however, the fact that he has collected inheritances from his aged "patients" is not necessarily evidence that he had hastened their deaths. In fact, reasonable doubt exists that Gustav had done anything other than prolong lives; and, after hearing Gustav's story, Zweig arranges for Gustav to elude arrest. In the end, Zweig loftily defends his decision by claiming that Gustav was a visionary instead of a criminal. Zweig's faith redeems Gustav, and he allows Gustav to escape because he believes that Gustav might still find the way to save all mankind.

Necessary Doubt received the usual double verdict: guilty of Wilsonian recklessness but innocent by virtue of earnestness. The *Times* reviewer wrote that "the whole odd mixture of miscellaneous erudition and casual flim-flam does somehow add up. Partly this is because of the audacity of it all, the sheer cheek. Partly it is because of Mr. Wilson's persistence in search of significance, even here. But basically it is because he continues to try to find out what is really important in life."[2] Wilson was commended for "narrative energy that makes the reader forgive him the detective story nonsense . . ."[3] but also condemned for the fact that "philosophical dabblings cannot disguise its basically antique apparatus."[4]

Critical opinion of the purely literary aspects of the work concerned Wilson less than occasional failures to perceive the novelist's ulterior motives. One serious reviewer did appreciate Wilson's "game" and saw clearly that the purpose of the work was not to entertain but to inform. He wrote: "While Wilson, the pretended 'square,' is playing the Sherlocking game strictly according to Doyle, the real Mr. Wilson is asking: How can men, caught up in the dizzy evolutions of the 20th century free themselves from obsolete habit patterns without plunging into moral chaos?" The reviewer felt, however, that Wilson's question was better than his answers. Yet he also qualified his verdict nicely: "It is not belittling — just a measure of the problem and its pertinence — to say that Mr. Wilson's question is better than his answers."[5] Knowledge, however, follows the proper asking of clearly stated questions. Furthermore, the answers must perforce be delayed when the questions probe the future as well as the present and the past. In his next novel, Wilson continues to ask big questions and to hazard answers — sometimes incautiously but always pertinently.

II The Glass Cage

Designated as an "unconventional detective story," *The Glass Cage* (1966)[6] is a version of the genre adapted to Wilson's purpose of promoting his philosophy. A solitude-loving authority on the work of William Blake, with the romantic name of Damon Reade, is enticed into playing detective when he learns of a Blake-quoting murderer whose bloody deeds have so far eluded conventional investigations. Reade clearly shows his Outsider-heritage and is responsive to the poetic visions of Blake. He also believes that he understands what makes certain people commit murder. Theorizing that murderers do their violent deeds as an attempt to break out of the "glass cage" of autism and that any violence, to one desperately in need of a breakthrough, is better than none, Reade has reasoned that frustrated murderers try to commit suicide sooner or later. They finally conclude that it is better to kill themselves than not to kill at all!

When Reade and a friend decide to test Reade's theories about the identity of the Blake-quoting murderer, they begin by investigating hospital records of attempted suicide. When the patterning of events allowable in fiction turns an improbability into a lucky hit, the murderer is identified. He appears to be so clever that he will never be brought to justice, but that is a minor point, for justice as such is not a concern of Wilson's scholar-turned-detective. The detecting is what counts to Reade — the intuition, later verified, of the existence of something other than superficial reality.

The "plot" of *The Glass Cage* is complicated but never so deliberately complex as in standard detective stories. No tricks are introduced just for the sake of throwing the reader off the path which leads to the truth, and the reader is always encouraged to confront ideological issues rather than to solve mysteries. The murderer, with whom Reade eventually develops a deep personal relationship which confounds friendship and therapy with identification, is the obvious suspect. He is a subtly disturbed fellow of impressive physique and frustrated life impulses, a man who has never learned how to satisfy the needs of his big body. As for Reade, he — like Gerard Sorme in *Ritual in the Dark* — intuitively understands killers; and, also like Gerard, he becomes a psychological if not legal accomplice after the fact when he refuses to summon authorities, who would only botch the affair.

Early in the novel Reade is established as sensitive and moody: he is bored and eager by turns and always sexually restrained. Reade detests fools, and he insists on discipline not only in himself but in others. When necessary, he can empty his mind of ideas and concentrate on emptiness. He is more or less engaged to Sarah, the fifteen-year-old ward of an eccentric bookseller, Urien Lewis. One evening Reade discusses his interest in the Blakean murderer with Sarah's guardian. At the insistence of Sarah, he goes to bed with her that night. His equivocal response to the girl is typical of the Outsider-syndrome. Like many of Wilson's protagonists, he is gentle — sexually acquiescent but not eager.

The use to which Wilson puts Reade's friendship with Lewis and his ward is contrived; however, what might be a failure of craft in a more subtle novelist is effective in this instance, because the design of the plot was meant to remain subordinate to the ideas being promoted. The novelist makes it clear that there is something evil in the relationship between the old bookseller and the attractive teenager, Sarah, who explains to Reade that Lewis is "kinky." Such kinkiness, Wilson implies, results from frustrated creative impulses. In a dialogue between Lewis and Reade, the novelist has the two probe relevant philosophical topics, including the significance of Reade's work. Lewis makes paranoid accusations against Reade, and the novelist thus puts the delicately balanced conscience of Reade on the record. Not surprisingly, Reade's defenses sound much like those of Colin Wilson himself when Reade insists that he can write books about the modern crisis while living the life of a hermit. Endorsing Whitehead's respect for intuition and showing how he himself logically progressed from Blake to Whitehead, Reade predicts the arguments of Wilson's later essays in which philosophy is called upon to restore meaning to the universe. After this interval of philosophical discourse, the story quickly resumes its concerns with how a brutal murderer may be identified, apprehended, and understood.

Reade's investigation includes consulting a local wizard who selects from an assortment of letters that Reade has received during a period of years from Blake enthusiasts the one most likely to have been written by a murderer. Following this clue, Reade gets in touch with an Oliver Bryce, an estate agent in Kensington Church Street, London. He also looks up his old friend Kit Butler, an avant-garde composer, and rents a room in the same building in which Butler lives, near the Portobello Road in Notting Hill. Kit Butler's casual creativity contrasts with Reade's disciplined rigor. Butler is a successful womanizer as well as an experimental composer. He responds to Reade's interest in the Blake-quoting murderer and by chance is able to help Reade. For example, because Butler *happens* to patronize writers and *happens* to be giving a party that very evening, Reade is soon mingling with characters who interest him.

After investigating several more leads, Reade intuitively knows the *how* of the murders he is trying to solve; for the answer is in himself: "Then, abruptly, the central facts became clear: guilt, obsession, and the need for purification" (100). After this realization, the story immediately picks up narrative speed; and Reade and Butler soon concentrate on a suspect, a Gaylord Sundheim, whose late father, a Blake scholar and enthusiast, had required his son to memorize long passages of poetry.

When Reade calls on Sundheim ostensibly to discuss Blake with him, Sundheim shows Reade his pet, a boa constrictor in a glass cage. He exhibits the snake proudly as what he himself would like to be: "Sleeps all day. No problems. No nerves" (138). Reade's first impression of Sundheim is that he could not be a murderer; but, as the evidence against Sundheim begins to grow, Reade yields to the possibility while still rationalizing to himself that Sundheim, even if he has committed the murders, is not really a criminal but an artist. Butler, who objects, argues that, although Sundheim may not be an ordinary criminal, he certainly ought to be stopped from killing people. Not interested in that point, Reade asks for more decisive encounters with Sundheim before accusing him.

A dramatic sequence of events soon involves Reade in quayside violence and in a visit to Sundheim's secret pad over a slaughterhouse, where he confirms the fact that Sundheim has committed a series of brutal murders. Sundheim eagerly defends himself as one of the "new men" overendowed with energy which he has had no socially acceptable way to release. That evening Reade watches Sundheim beat two Negroes and attempt to rape a prostitute; nevertheless, Reade spends the night unarmed in the murderer's pad over the slaughterhouse, a handy place to cut up bodies. In the morning, when Reade returns home, he discovers that a general alarm has been sounded for the apprehension of Sundheim. The story ends in a cinematic cliché, with Reade bravely defying the holed-up Sundheim's gunfire as he alone enters the besieged room where Sundheim has taken his stand. The final dialogue between Sundheim and Reade, while the police momentarily hold their fire, extracts the last bit of significance from Sundheim's crimes and Reade's interest in them.

Reade tells Sundheim that he is now committed to Sundheim's side. When the police break in, Sundheim surrenders his gun to Reade and himself to the police without resistance; for he has been convinced by Reade that not enough evidence exists to convict him. Reade tells the police officials nothing more than is already known, and he predicts that Sundheim will not be convicted in court — that he will instead commit himself to a mental hospital and then probably kill himself within two years. This prediction is as far as Wilson is willing to go in providing a moral ending to his parable, although the final image of the narrative focuses on the snake as it prepares to shed its old skin, no doubt thus symbolizing hope through renewal.

Wilson openly intended to advance his ideas in *The Glass Cage*, and the novel is designated "an unconventional detective story" on the title page. Thus it would not be appropriate to evaluate it as a regular member of the class of thrillers in which suspense and violence are sensationalized in order to titillate jaded readers. Wilson himself has classified *The Glass Cage* along with *Ritual in the Dark* as a "crime novel," by which he doubtless means that crime is both the theme and the action, and that the criminals and the crime detectors are, respectively, the protagonists and the antagonists.

One professional evaluation of the work suggested that it would probably be most successful for a "discriminating audience."[7] Such an audience, however, tended to find the novel either too sensational or too simplistic.[8] One London reviewer called Wilson's prose "lumpy" and faulted the "dully predictable conclusion."[9] Although it is true that the prose is not distinguished, it is, when read with the intention of understanding the narrative rather than searching for subtle aesthetic effects, adequate to its purpose. Again the verdict of "dullness" is more nearly a function of misreading — hunting for surprise endings, for example — than the failure of the author to meet his responsibility to the genre. Few readers were willing to cooperate with Wilson's emphasis on ideas.

After *The Glass Cage*, Wilson began to experiment with science fiction, a genre perhaps better suited to his ulterior motives. Logical extrapolations from the present to the future which are characteristic of good science fiction liberate the reader from the need to work at suspending his disbelief, for he *knows* that these events could not yet have occurred.

III The Mind Parasites

In a candidly personal preface Wilson tells how he came to write *The Mind Parasites* (1967): "It so happens that the Lovecraft tradition is largely my own. I feel more at home with books than with people. I take a great delight in adding authenticity to my fiction by piling-in the results of my reading, and by working out elaborate myths of metaphysical systems."[10] The "Lovecraft tradition," which has become something of a cult, projects an elaborate and completely invented mythology as serious if not downright profound. Wilson was admittedly much influenced by Lovecraft's stories[11] and by his enthusiasm for the supernatural and the macabre which was based on his serious concern over the limitations of ordinary science and ordinary consciousness. Believing that fear is the strongest human emotion as well as the most ancient one, Lovecraft also supposed that fear of the unknown is the strongest kind of fear. This strong fear explains the appeal of trying to predict the future and to peer into the supernatural — both of which are only dimly visible, if at all, to ordinary perceptions. Lovecraft's defense of his fantastic myths about the old gods who will awaken in the future and about the old fears that will almost destroy mankind parallels Wilson's reasons for devoting his career to attempts to penetrate various barriers between potential man and potentiated man.

Lovecraft's theory is summarized in an essay written in 1926 and reprinted in 1965. Entitled "Supernatural Horror in Literature," the essay defines the rationale for exploiting incredible events in fiction. Lovecraft wrote: "For those who relish speculation regarding the future, the tale of supernatural horror provides an interesting field. Combated by a mounting wave of plodding realism, cynical flippancy, and sophisticated disillusionment, it is yet encouraged by a parallel tide of growing mysticism, as developed both through the fatigued reaction of 'occultists' and religious fundamentalists against materialistic discovery and through the stimulation of wonder and fancy by such enlarged vistas and broken barriers as modern science has given us with its intra-atomic chemistry, advancing astrophysics, doctrines of relativity, and probings into biology and human thought."[12]

Wilson hoped to implement Lovecraft's vision with his own additional probings. He was immediately defensive, however, in the prefatory statement to his new novel. Of the "flaccid prose" of the opening pages of *The Mind Parasites*, Wilson says that they were supposed to be parody. He adds: "It didn't come off; but what the hell. I'd rather get on with another book than tinker about with it" (xxi). Such honesty, although it cannot redeem all artistic sins, is certainly disarming. Even hostile critics might be tempted to read the work for those much vaunted "ideas" rather than for the more subtle pleasures to be had from fine prose.

The Mind Parasites moves from a solemn epigraph by Bertrand

Russell about "the vastness and the fearful passionless force of non-human beings" through fantastic extrapolations to an intense climax. One of the ways to make an incredible proposition credible is to move it into the future, and *The Mind Parasites* is a projection of a conflict many years from now with the Tsathogguans, wily microscopic parasites that menace civilization by infecting the best minds of the age. The time is 2007, and the renowned scientist Professor Gilbert Austin has disappeared. His "story," put together from his papers, tapes, and reports, is announced as Volume III of the *Cambridge History of the Nuclear Age*. The narrative begins with a transcription of a tape recording made by Gilbert Austin before his disappearance from the earth, apparently to join the space police. He has taken the "evolutionary leap," leaving his records behind as guides for other men.

According to the recording, Karel Weisman, Austin's friend of thirty years, had just committed suicide, leaving behind a letter requesting that Austin take charge of Weisman's "scientific papers." At the time, Austin was deeply involved in his own archaeological research and preoccupied with certain new findings. "There can be no possible doubt that the Tsathogguans were awaiting my return," his voice on the tape explains, "waiting to see what I did. And luckily, my head was full of archaeology. My mind was floating gently in the immense seas of the past, lulled in the currents of history" (15). The parasites, presumably, could not penetrate Austin's consciousness while he was thinking. According to the tape, Austin did, however, finally confront the dreaded parasites, the enemies of essential man; and in that confrontation he achieved the liberating understanding which endowed him with extended power to act in behalf of mankind.

The details of the plot are clever, often nicely fitted together, but sometimes far-out even for this genre. Anyway, the parasites may be understood as symbolic manifestations of an evil power which had become increasingly apparent throughout history, particularly by the end of the eighteenth century, an era Austin describes as a critical one: "And suddenly, we are in an age of darkness, an age where men of genius no longer create like gods. Instead, they struggle as if in the grip of an invisible octopus. The century of suicide begins. In fact, modern history begins, the age of defeat and neurosis" (57 - 58). The reference is to Romanticism and its correlatives: suicide, depression, madness, tuberculosis, cancer, and other psychosomatic diseases.

Austin has wondered what man would be like if he could banish these parasites. The answer, he believes, was first glimpsed only in infrequent moments during peak experiences which were later extended into durable periods of creativity as man took up the "legacy of Husserl" and liberated his "inner-powers" (67). Eventually, in the projected time of the narrative, the critical battle against the parasites was waged by Austin and his friend Reich, who used phenomenological techniques. Because neither was a philosopher, they had no trouble with preconceptions. They understood Husserl's ideas intuitively, and they carefully trained a few others to battle the parasites with them. They knew, however, that intelligence was not enough in this fight; they had to learn to explore consciousness itself, for it was there that the parasites hid.

This simplified version of Husserlian phenomenology is not bad phenomenology. Phenomenology, whatever it may finally *be*, is not necessarily complicated. Referring to the "knack of using the mind properly" (82), Austin's recorded voice explains: "It is a matter of breaking a habit that human beings have acquired over millions of years: of giving all their attention to the outside world, and thinking of 'imagination' as a kind of escapism, instead of recognizing that it is a brief excursion into the great unknown countries of the mind. You had to get used to thinking how your mind worked. Not just your 'mind' in the ordinary sense, but your feelings and perceptions as well. I found that by far the most difficult thing, to begin with, was to realize that 'feeling' is just another form of perception" (82).

The innovative methodology in phenomenological analysis *is* phenomenology, which entails a rejection of the blinkered methodology of natural science. The phenomenologist can discover the mind parasites only because he has rejected the limitations of other methodologies. A conventional scientist searching for parasites observes his cultures, peers into his test tubes, watches for reactions, checks the variables that are *supposed* to vary, and holds constant those that are *supposed* to remain constant. Capricious parasites, since they are free to exist or not as they will, cannot be detected by those who must assume lawfulness in the subjects of their study. Willful capriciousness in subject matter, human or otherwise, is inimical to the procedures of ordinary science. It is clear then that Wilson's fantasy-parasites represent ordinary science, a methodology which has limited man's power to discover truth: "The aim of the parasites was to prevent human beings from arriving at their maximum powers, and they did this by 'jamming' the emotions, by blurring our feelings so that we failed to learn from them, and went around in a kind of mental fog" (84). The laboratory microbiologist could not find these parasites because he was blind to events other than those for which he had set up the experiment. But the new man will not only locate the parasites but also defeat them eventually, one presumes, with Colin Wilson's help.

Because the phenomenological approach to reality is appropriate to science fiction, *The Mind Parasites* has a built-in authenticity. The fantastic can be literally true to phenomenologists, while the scientifically demonstrable, as in physics, is assumed to be merely an artifact of the limitations of the "natural viewpoint" of so-called reality. Wilson's fantasy has been compared to H. G. Wells's extrapolations from observable facts. Praised as up-dated Jules Verne in England, the novel is a favorite among Wilson-specialists but generally not taken seriously by literary critics. Wilson himself has classified it along with *The Sex Diary of Gerard Sorme* as one of his partly tongue-in-cheek works. It is certainly less fastidiously written than his several later novels despite Wilson's insistence that he *meant* to parody tediousness in the opening pages. Good parodies of bad writing must perforce be more interesting than the originals or the effort of the parodist has been misdirected. Parody should reveal weakness in the original rather than in itself.

IV The Philosopher's Stone

In a second parable qua novel, *The Philosopher's Stone* (1969),[13] Wilson conjectures that the era which preceded man was dominated by supernatural forces called the "Old Ones" who created man as part of an experiment in invading matter. Man appeared first as a hairless, retarded ape designed to function as a tool only. The Old Ones were deficient in precision and overflowing with undifferentiated power and thus needed an instrument to carry out their plans.

Knowledge of these past events comes through time-vision liberated by a new kind of "philosopher's stone." A microscopic bit of special metal inserted in the frontal lobe of the brain stimulates the imagination. Eventually those who undergo the cortical operation learn how to expand consciousness without the mediation of the bit of metal. The operation only facilitates a will to potentiate what is already there.

Like *The Mind Parasites, The Philosopher's Stone* is an "apocalyptic parable" reaching for existential realism.[14] Just as yesterday's wonders become today's commonplaces, an imaginative twist can change today's commonplaces into tomorrow's wonders. The perennial popularity of the time-machine fantasy is related to the psychological fact that man is a remembering animal wont to project a future in terms of either a positive or negative image of the past or of the immediate present. The scientist assumes that tomorrow must be what today and all yesterdays made it, but Colin Wilson takes never-ending pains to deny such an assumption while not abandoning rigorous thinking. Combining cognition with mysticism, he functions most effectively in that area of science fiction in which fantasy emerges logically from facts.

In *The Philosopher's Stone*, negative forces which obstruct man's perceiving faculties are just as real as those which facilitate the imagination. Wilson has never doubted the validity of obstructing processes nor the reality of human faculties which are being obstructed. There are many roads to a given end, and, although neither mind parasites nor potent metal catalysts have yet been verified in the laboratory, their "reality" is inferable without outrage from the way people behave. Also, in his role as phenomenologist, Wilson feels justified in using personal experience as authority more often than an ordinary scientist would feel comfortable doing; thus, it is important to stress Wilson's unwavering confidence in himself. An authority is one whom one can trust, and Wilson invariably trusts himself.

The Philosopher's Stone is a kind of memoir. Beginning with the narrator's birth in 1942 in a Nottinghamshire village (close to where D. H. Lawrence was born), the story first projects the time line into the future via the usual devices of noting books and events in a "past" dated in the reader's future. The narrator, earnest truth-seeker Howard Lester, cites one of his own works first published in 1972 and reprinted in 1975 — a truth that is, of course, immediately beyond verification. The major conflict in Howard's early life is between his love of science and his love of music. Subject to the usual familial expectations that he should *be* something, young Howard realizes that he mostly respects unconventional values. He is lucky, however, to acquire an enlightened patron early enough in life to save him the time and energy that less fortunate (and less fictitious) persons waste in working for a living. As Wilson did, Howard decides against a formal university education; instead, he reads widely on his own and experiments in his own laboratory.

Howard spends his days in the British Museum Reading Room searching for ways to expand human consciousness in order to prolong life. He concludes that any event which penetrates indifference and changes the thresholds of perception may potentiate vitality in those who know how to direct the released energy. Although animals experience ecstasy, only human consciousness is capable of directing itself; that is, human consciousness is both intentional and rational. With the help of a friend, Sir Henry Littleway, Howard begins a series of experiments which climax in a dramatic breakthrough when the two scientists discover that they can induce "value experiences" by inserting a tiny electrode made of "Neumann's alloy" into the prefrontal lobe of the human cortex; and the effect of the operation is like putting the brain into gear.

The experimenters operate on themselves and learn that, once accelerated, their awareness remains that way. As they realize that such increased awareness can not only probe the deepest secrets of human consciousness but also has psychic and mystical correlatives, they learn to use their senses to let impressions in rather than to keep them out. They define the imagination that they have intensified as "the ability to grasp the reality of factors not actually present to the senses . . . a power to reach out beyond present reality just as radar can penetrate clouds" (133).

With their heightened imaginative powers carefully directed, Howard and his friend quickly learn how to perceive the past as clearly as if it were the present. They are able to fill out the first impression of an archaeological artifact with all the circumstances that once surrounded it. At first, the experience is merely pleasant, such as waking up each day with an excited feeling of anticipation. But soon the two experimenters sense hostile forces trying to prevent them from utilizing their increased awareness to penetrate the "Great Secret" and other primal mysteries. Opposition via vibrations and statistically improbable accidents frustrates their attempts to search out the ur-springs of life. Howard especially feels strong evil forces when he visits Stonehenge and tries to reconstruct imaginatively its history.

On the positive side, Howard continues to have peak experiences in which he knows "that all human beings can enter into a close, deep communion if they will make the effort to break through the normal barriers of pettiness and self-absorption" (235). As the quest assumes a religious quality, the struggle between the experimenters and the dark powers that are reluctant to have their secrets revealed is intensified; for good is attacking evil. Finally Howard and Littleway discover a crystal divining bowl that once belonged to the priest K'tholo, a mighty prophet who had lived for a half million years and who had survived the destruction of the "Mu civilization" and the terrible catastrophes which destroyed the underground cities of the gods and the above ground civilizations of their humanoid servants. Through time-vision, the experimenters uncover all K'tholo's secrets.

As Howard and his friend face their own future, they know what they have to do. Although they are the first new men, they have only temporarily thwarted the powers of darkness. They know that the Old Ones, who put themselves to sleep in order to escape the destruction brought about by their having refined their conscious powers at the expense of the unconscious, will not sleep forever. When they awaken, men must be ready for them; and, to be so, men must become "a society of Masters"; however, they must awaken the Old Ones cautiously: "For nothing is more clear . . . than that man will soon need the Old Ones as much as they once needed him" (313).

The parable ends on a note of warning which seems to endorse a creative power-elite, but the "program" is really open to all: "Man should possess an infinite appetite for life. It should be self-evident to him, all the time, that life is superb, glorious, endlessly rich, infinitely desirable" (314). Obviously, this vision of a "brave new world" is really not so fantastic; for recent experiments with sensitivity training and chemically-induced "trips" into increased awareness have begun to validate Wilson's vision.[15]

The Mind Parasites and *The Philosopher's Stone* were both consciously crafted by Wilson in the same tradition and use the legendary framework created by the master himself, the late H. P. Lovecraft. Noting that neither Wilson's theme nor his hero has changed, one reviewer evaluated the work as pretentious and derivative, with the author "genuflecting before G. B. Shaw."[16] On the other hand, he was simultaneously praised for his "careful narrative style" and "his determination to be at all times the most polymathic of writers."[17] Although Wilson had taken care — more than usual — to edit and check his facts, one reviewer complained that "anyone with a specialized knowledge of any of the areas covered is bound to find his toes severely trodden on."[18] In an age of specialization a Renaissance man might well blunder into amateurism in more than one area of his interests. At this point in his career Wilson begins to suffer from the comprehensiveness of his search for knowledge as well as to benefit from his growing maturity.

Impatient with not knowing everything, he has, however, had more time to learn more and more. Fairly viewed as a product of his own quest for his own kind of philosopher's stone, the work is thoughtful, modestly probing, and justifiably speculative in terms of its genre, which specifies that extrapolations from present facts into future possibilities shall be probable although not necessarily highly probable — and in all aspects at least possible under certain circumstances.

V Lingard

In Wilson's next work of fiction, he returns to the "crime novel." *Lingard* (1970), called *The Killer* in the first British edition,[19] is closely related to two earlier novels by Wilson, *Ritual in the Dark* and *The Glass Cage.* Wilson was convinced that Truman Capote's best-selling *In Cold Blood* was not really an adequate example of the "non-fictional novel" so he decided to write a better one. He also intended to refine his projection of the Outsider as a violent man caught between the inability either to rationalize or to potentiate his violence. By this time, Wilson is sure that suppressed creativity motivates criminals as much as constructive violence motivates artists. Perhaps as a defense against predictable negative reactions to his new work Wilson includes an introduction in which he confesses his uncertainty about the result of his "experiment." Asserting that, in any event, this book "is the closest I can get to it," Wilson implies that he would welcome even hostility as evidence of some understanding of what he is trying to do. Knowing that his novel exploits sensation and sexuality, he is even willing to risk having the novel denounced as "a shilling shocker." He explains that he has deliberately not courted easy suspension of disbelief through the use of clever rhetorical devices.

Without this statement of intent, Wilson's "failure" would resemble the rationalization of a schoolboy who has been downgraded for a platitudinous essay and who *later* claims that he meant the paper to illustrate trite diction. Intentionality must somehow announce itself early enough in any act to be beyond suspicion. Establishing the difference between first and second degree murder, for example, is not always easy. In defense of Wilson's method, it may be pointed out that protesting before, during, and after the act that his act is more significant than it may at first appear to be, is itself part of the act. Failure thus can become part of succeeding in achieving the intention of not succeeding. The method at least avoids false meekness, and it at best promotes a feeling of faith in the writer's conviction that, despite possible technical failures, he is still more nearly right than wrong.

Like Arthur Lingard, the killer in his story, Wilson is himself an example of the category he is promoting — "the right man." He borrowed the phrase from science-fiction writer A. E. Van Vogt, and he cites as examples of extremely "right men" Hitler, Stalin, Mao Tse Tung, and Khrushchev. These extreme types, however, are less significant to Wilson than more moderately "right men," who, Wilson believes, are all artists: "Any artist of high individuality is saying, essentially: '*I am right.* This is what life is really like' " (282). Although some of these so-called *right* people must perforce be wrong, since they violently disagree with one another, the intensity of their stand rather than its ultimate validity intrigues Wilson.

For Wilson, it is but a short step from the studio to the jail, from art to crime. Lingard is a composite portrait of a killer, for he is both an Outsider and a "right man"; and, of course, he is more talented and stronger-willed than the average man. His actions dramatize the limits of two paradigms: he is both violent criminal and creative artist. The whole work is addressed no less than to "the fundamental problem of our society [which] is to learn to distinguish the 'right men' and induce them to develop inner checks". Wilson hoped the novel "might be regarded as a wilful complication of the problem: an attempt to point out that 'right men' are not necessarily and completely wrong" (286).

The main character is a composite one from cases cited in Wilson's *Encyclopedia* and *Casebook*. Lingard's childhood, Wilson informs the reader, came from Kürten; his burglaries and his underwear fetishism from William Heirens; his "imaginative instability" from Hans Van Zorn. Most of his psychiatric symptoms were "lifted wholesale from Medard Boss's *Psychoanalysis and Daseinanalysis*, Erwin Straus's *Phenomenological Psychology*, Robert Lindner's *The Fifty Minute Hour*, Frederick Wertham's *The Show of Violence* . . . and Ludwig Binswanger's *Case of Ellen West*" (5). With such a heritage, Lingard has to carry a heavy burden of theory as well as many bad habits.

The story begins on June 19, 1967, with the first meeting between a psychiatrist, Dr. Kahn, and the prisoner-patient, Lingard. A series of flashbacks related to the psychiatrist's investigation of the case fill in the background of both Lingard and his doctor, Samuel Kahn, author of a popular paperback study of criminals. Although Kahn reports that prisoners generally like to talk with him, Lingard, who is serving the last years of an eight-year sentence for the second-degree murder of an old man, is not at first very cooperative. In fact, he often appears to withdraw into a catatonic trance. "Suddenly," the narrator-psychiatrist confesses, "all my scientific and human curiosity was aroused. I wanted to know" (15). After ascertaining that Lingard is not intellectually subnormal as other doctors had thought, Kahn shrewdly studies one of the books Lingard has borrowed from the prison library. The killer has been reading an account of nineteenth-century terrorists called *Romantic Exiles*. He is obviously not an ordinary psychopath.

Kahn pursues several lines of inquiry, ranging from ordinary sleuthing to intuitions concerning suspects. Although Lingard is in some respects a simple clinical case — specifically, a paranoid with delusions of power as well as of persecution — his several killings have been far from standard. Lingard's description of the "forces of evil" which he believes are after him correlates with his sexual fantasies and imaginative murders, and his sex life has been both colorful and promiscuous. He has indulged in incest, buggering, fellatio, and other less common perversions. Lingard's sister, upon whom he was "fixated" as a lad, was a nymphomaniac; and most of the boy's precocious sex experiences were traumatic. His dissatisfaction with his drab environment and his intermittent recourse to highly charged fantasies provided by his reading and his own imagination combined with his tendency toward epilepsy had finally doomed him.

In pursuit of his point, however, Wilson does not neglect to identify a goodly portion of willfulness in Lingard's fate. Thus Kahn is made to speculate that Lingard's antisocial behavior is best accounted for by "third-force" psychologists, such as Viktor Frankl, Abraham Maslow, and Carl Rogers, all of whom recognize the importance of satisfying "higher needs." The syndrome fits Lingard; for, a lover of crime for the sake of excitement rather than loot, his "creative acts" have included seducing his cousin, killing a man who seduced him, and disemboweling assorted females. The last activity correlates with the period in Lingard's life when fantasies about Jack the Ripper had supplanted his daydreams about other heroes. Other symptoms of creative maturity in the criminal include embellishing his murders with ritual mutilations of the victims. Without these extra attractions, the killings might have been humdrum affairs and thus not imaginatively satisfying!

The Killer was denounced by one reviewer as "closer to pornography than to a novel."[20] The intention of the novelist was certainly not honored by such a verdict. More importantly, the mootness of the work pertains to the relative success of Wilson's attempt to create a "composite figure"[21] out of several "real" cases. The so-called nonfiction novel is not quite a respectable genre, contradicting itself, as it were, in its two essences: telling the truth and making up a story. Wilson's effort to refine the genre by making up the truth as well, is honorable insofar as he does not conceal his sources and the extent to which he has altered and combined them. Wilson's interest in murders and murderers may seem decadent to those who categorize human behavior as lawful or unlawful. As a philosopher concerned with motives as well as with effects, however, Wilson seriously explores his far from trivial theories about how violence such as murder is related to creativity and how sexuality often underlies both. After the insights of Freud, Wilson seems justified in taking long second looks at all that has been claimed for the impulses to make love and to kill as well as the complementary impulses to be loved and to be killed. *Lingard* is a readable experiment in combining speculation with fact to produce the kind of novel that can be trusted as reliable because it is based on careful research as well as on imagination.

VI The God of the Labyrinth

The God of the Labyrinth (1970)[22] is another experiment and is also unabashedly didactic. It complements the Gerard Sorme of *Ritual in the Dark* and *The Sex Diary* with an eighteenth-century rake named Esmond Donelly to form a double narrator-questor. Both Gerard and Esmond are incredible enough separately; together, they exceed credibility at an accelerating rate as the novelist tries to demonstrate that Gerard, a twentieth-century sexual connoisseur, and Esmond, an eighteenth-century sexual athlete, are one and the same person.

The demonstration is supported by the widest and wildest implications of such events as multiple orgasms and other sexual pyrotechnics. Never before has Wilson been so enthusiastic about the simple joys of sex as well as its more spiritual coordinates. Wilson here has gone far beyond D. H. Lawrence, for example, in glorifying sexuality; but, be that as it may, the novel begins quietly enough. Gerard Sorme, now a mature intellectual, is jotting down entries in his journal. He is in the middle of a wearying lecture tour. Married for seven years, he is the father of one child; and, although sexually experienced beyond the marital bed, he is still capable of the highest physical pleasure with his wife.

Two days after the campus lecture in Oregon, Gerard flies to New York. There he is offered five thousand dollars by a literary agent to write an introduction to an edition of an Esmond Donelly's intimate confessions, which were allegedly unearthed by the promoter. Gerard's reputation as a pornographer, established after the publication of his diary, had recommended him for the job. He is also offered a ten-thousand-dollar bonus if he can either find other writings by Donelly or forge sufficient documents to fill a complete book.

Soon complications, which are too intricate to summarize, precipitate Gerard into a tangle of intrigue, including many bedroom adventures. Accepting the offer to write a book ostensibly by Donelly that would compete with such erotica as de Sade's *Justine* and the anonymous work entitled *My Secret Life*, Gerard begins an adventure which takes him to a neurotic descendant of Donelly, who supplies him with extracts from the rake's diary that seem more nearly authentic than the material he had been given by the literary agent. In passing, it should be mentioned that extracts from manuscripts allegedly written by Donelly are included in Wilson's novel. They are, of course, themselves clever imitations of early erotica.

Gerard begins to have déjà-vu experiences early in his quest. The trail which he hoped would lead him to more Donelly manuscripts, as well as to a clearer understanding of the function of sex in promoting increased awareness, becomes more and more complicated. His adventures, however, are really more devious than dangerous and do not achieve suspenseful peaks. While Gerard observes, participates, and performs, Wilson lectures.

In the course of his research Gerard flagellates the descendant of Esmond Donelly when requested, remaining fairly detached while he intensifies his philosophical commitment that the man's "perversions" are "proof of the freedom of the human spirit. All animals shrink from pain," Gerard reasons. "Donelly had deliberately acquired the opposite attitude. He had chosen that pain should be a value, and he made it a value — something he enjoyed" (48). Gerard sees "a touch of the saint" in all deviants. Moreover, Gerard realizes that he has not only begun to identify with Donelly psychologically but also to equal Esmond's sexual endurance if not yet the full measure of his profligacy. At this point, Wilson delicately balances his protagonist-propagandist between sanity and insanity. Momentarily, Gerard hesitates; he battles with his reluctance to surrender and to accept his dual nature by acknowledging that he is also Esmond.

By the time Gerard is adjusted to his double consciousness, he is deep into several new adventures in which he simultaneously plays both Esmond and himself. He participates in an orgy as part of an experiment in consciousness expansion in which the objective is to control sex rather than to stimulate it. Soon he stumbles upon a cult, the Sect of the Phoenix, which specializes in sexual excesses. As Esmond-Gerard, he discovers that he can perform sexual feats no man had ever dreamed of. In one of his final epiphanies, he experiences himself as the god of that sexual labyrinth all men want to explore, a magnificent stud ready, eager, and able to service countless priestesses.

The God of the Labyrinth asks for the license to be passionately didactic as well as deliberately alienating. In Wilson's own terms, it functions successfully: it leaves the reader with a residuum of noninvolved concern which does not dissipate at the close of the tale but which hopefully increases as one begins to think about it all. Nevertheless, the novel was reviewed both acridly and wearily. The thesis was said to be disturbing. Also, Sorme and his "ideas" were no longer new. The message of the novel is that liberating the spirit and mind is man's main business, but the fact that liberation is here correlated with sexuality opened Wilson to attack.

The *Times* reviewer understood the novel well enough when he wrote that Wilson's "theme" has to do with "sex as a provider of vast intellectual and spiritual luminosity which cannot, but should be, sustained. . . ." But the reviewer revealed his distaste with the theme and with Wilson's handling of it in his concluding remark: "Everybody in this novel seems ready to go to bed with the first person who comes along, or at least to discuss the oddities of their sex-lives at the drop of a pantie-girdle."[23] Still another reviewer charged that, although the novel starts well enough, "it degenerates rapidly into esoteric . . . hokum."[24] Disgusted with the pornographic details in the novel, one critic denounced Wilson as "a seeker after enlightenment who faces life with his mental eyes shut."[25]

Such denunciations by British intellectuals may signify more than praise. Remembering how violently Thomas Hardy's last novel, *Jude the Obscure*, was attacked in England and how the novelist was reviled as dirty and incompetent, one should be alerted to the possible information contained in ill-natured invective. Truth-tellers are always vulnerable; but this statement is not meant to say, of course, that all who are attacked are truth-tellers. Hardy as novelist did not survive the attack on *Jude;* Wilson, however, is an authority on how to survive both fame and infamy; but only time and his total canon can prepare the final verdict on him. His next novel is another experiment — in science fiction this time.

VII The Black Room

Anyone who writes and publishes as prolifically as Colin Wilson sooner or later partially repeats himself. In all fairness, however, it must be said that Wilson has usually created significant variations of his original themes. Convinced, to the point of obsession, that most human beings are deliberately unwilling to penetrate the haze which neither comforts nor kills them, Wilson has ceaselessly searched for ways to persuade them to arise and fight. *The Black Room* (1971)[26] is the most intensified projection to date of Wilson's conviction that human consciousness still slumbers. In it, Wilson combines science-fiction techniques with the conventions of the so-called "spy novel"; and the result is a sturdy hybrid suitable for Wilson's purpose, which is once again to shock the reader into increased awareness by informing him of certain important facts and involving him in the implications of those facts. The work can be read as the third part of a trilogy of which the first two parts are *The Philosopher's Stone* and *The Mind Parasites.*

Orwell's *1984* and Huxley's *Brave New World* had spelled out a list of warnings with which traditional humanists were comfortable. Men must watch out, Orwell and Huxley had said, lest they lose the freedom to be themselves. No matter how tawdry or tacky their selves may be, they are at least their own — poor things, but their own. In contrast, such a mild stand infuriates Wilson; he resists with all his self-taught learning and his self-earned independence any suffering-unto-death resignation. Wilson's quest is not for the good old self that got lost when the world began to be too much with us; he searches, instead, for a new self which must be radically discovered and perfected.

A "black room" is a useful device for cutting off information from the outside. In both a light-proof and a sound-proof room, an individual *inside* the black room is outside the outside. Without the information about the outside world which he normally gets from variations in light and sound, a person confined inside the black room must rely on himself alone for evidence that he is still alive. A person in such a state either survives because he is sufficiently self-dependent to keep his awareness alive without evidence that he can still see or hear, or eventually capitulates to the blackness and the silence and "loses his mind." The paradigm is just right for Wilson's concerns; for, endorsing self-reliance rather than paternalisms of all kinds and believing passionately in the will to survive as essential, Wilson would minimize environmental factors. The idea of a black room in which a human subject could potentiate his identity rather than lose it begins as a metaphor, develops into a device for brainwashing, and ends up in Wilson's novel as a crisis experience in which "danger and difficulty unite the whole being" (290).

The novel is burdened with intrigue, spies, quasi-mad scientists, amoral females, and other gadgetry. That very burden, however, helps to separate the intellectual thrust of the book from the medium; for, in such novels, the medium is *not* the message. The medium remains strictly a medium, exploiting characters and plot to facilitate the message. In this case, the central character, Kit Butler, and the business-of-the-black room are efficiently meshed. Kit, a composer and music critic, is bright, sensitive, and concerned both professionally and compassionately with the problem of awareness; and he bears witness to Wilson's personal concerns. Kit is eventually involved with a group of people who are variously interested in the black-room phenomenon. In the final incident in the book, Kit becomes a guest-prisoner of a group of international conspirators vaguely dedicated to saving the world. Their leader, a former Nazi, insists that Hitler is still alive in South America and that Hitler's powers, although obviously used for evil ends, were truly remarkable. Wilson implies that the final truth about Hitler and about the realms of international intrigue must be extrapolated from a few observables, for the truth about such truth is that it is always successfully concealed.

Kit Butler is an adventurer, a moderate drinker, not an athlete but physically brave. Creative and daring, he pushes outward. He is the nonfailed Outsider. As the plot in which Kit at first serves as a subject in black-room experiments moves into the international arena, Kit converses with the former Nazi at a high level of knowledge and concern. On the track of a mysterious "Station K," Kit blunders into a Utopian settlement somewhere in either Austria or Russia in which the members of the community, including seductive and graciously cooperative women, experiment without smut and lewdness with nudity and love.

By this time, spying has become the most powerful weapon in the world, for no bombs can be used effectively anymore. The only safe weapon against the enemy is knowledge of his whereabouts and intentions. Since any resort to bombing, for example, would destroy the whole world, information is of the essence. The thesis is compelling and frightening as Wilson posits it. The Nazi leader eventually explains to Kit that he believes it is possible to *create* greatness in men but that greatness is not necessarily innate; therefore, the most important concern of today's world should be how to promote heroic qualities in potential leaders. The final test of such superiority is "the power to withstand the black room" (276).

Fortunately, Kit has himself developed that power by deliberately intensifying the feeling of crisis while he is in the black room; conversely, he resists yielding to either passivity or panic. Since Kit's "concentration index" is phenomenal, the scientists who are involved in the building of greatness in men respect his theory about how he had achieved such heightened awareness. Soon Kit is the key figure in their experiments. After a series of incidents in which Kit demonstrates his victory over isolation, the novel ends quietly. Kit is participating in a dangerous mission with the members of the international spy-ring, who are determined to save the world. At the critical moment in the mission, the outcome of which the novelist leaves suspended, Kit has a "peak experience." Feeling both "affirmation and detachment," he stands waiting for the critical moment: "He was intensely aware of the night, of the trees, of the flowing water and the snow-covered stones at the edge of the stream, and also of his own identity suspended amongst these things. But it seemed unimportant whether he was there or elsewhere. It was as if he could make time stand still by an act of concentration" (347 - 48).

The Black Room is completely timely. Governments have begun seriously to use psychological procedures in training political leaders and intelligence gatherers. Any device for obtaining critical information is considered a justifiable weapon. The bugging of telephones and burglarizing of embassies is still child's play, however, compared to recent speculations of more sophisticated ways of invading personal privacies. Primitive kinds of brainwashing have been around a long time, but only recently has one begun to realize that effective brainwashing always erases the memory of having been brainwashed. Mind parasites and black rooms are no longer quite such fantastic concepts as they once seemed. Wilson's extrapolations are beginning to appear more prophetic than fanciful.

VIII *The Outsider as Novelist: Guilty or Innocent?*

Spinning tales to amuse idle readers or distract troubled readers from other problems has never been Wilson's intention — nor perhaps easily within his competence either. One can draw a line under *The Black Room* (1971) and add up the significance of Wilson's novels through the latter work and test the case for or against Wilson as a creative writer, being careful to assess the total impact of the works as well as the success or failure of individual items. This study has presented a representative sample of current critical reactions to the various novels, many of which indicate that Wilson's reputation as a novelist still suffers from the failure of some critics to perceive his intentions and evaluate his performances in that context. Wilson has intended to produce an *oeuvre*, a body of work which includes exposition, drama, criticism, and fiction as a battalion fighting against apathy and inertia. By the end of the 1960s Wilson saw clearly that if he was to attract readers at all he had to exploit the media that reach readers. In *The Black Room*, which is built squarely on the foundations of the Lovecraft tradition but which rises to its own height and breadth, Wilson intended a prophetic vision, one which would serve to warn the innocent and alert the lethargic to what is now known about how to control human beings and the dangers of misapplying such knowledge. Time will test the novel adequately, for it is competently written and makes few concessions to the needs of ordinary readers.

On the other hand, as it were, Wilson's urgency could not fail to motivate him to use more popular categories of fiction and above all more efficient media of communication. One of his most recent projects includes writing a series of twelve "mysteries" of the kind suitable for adaptation to television. The first of the series, ingenuously called *The Schoolgirl Murder Case* (1974),[27] combines Wilson's interest in crime with his research into the occult. It introduces an intrepid detective from Scotland Yard, Gregory Saltfleet, who doubtless will reappear in other volumes, for he is a carefully developed intelligence pursuing truth both intuitively and systematically — a typical Wilsonian construct. Despite Saltfleet's appeal as a masterful sleuth, other aspects of the work almost deliberately fail to follow the formula of the genre, which traditionally requires both real and false clues, numerous suspects, and elaborate explanations for how it all happened.

The Schoolgirl Murder Case, for example, throws away its most interesting character, Manfred Lytton, by introducing him as the second corpse — the first being the so-called schoolgirl who is revealed at once as an aging prostitute dressed to look young and pert for one of her clients, namely, Manfred Lytton. Lytton's taste in sex and other amusements was decadent, and by the time Saltfleet finds out who killed the prostitute and her customer, the reader is treated to a nice assortment of sadistic details. As in most of Wilson's detective novels it does not come as a surprise that the suspect really did do what he is suspected of, and this lack of real suspense may impair Wilson's success as a popular writer of thrillers for mass audiences. Also, the significance of the killings, involving the familiar Wilsonian emphases on passion and such strange combinations as joining "the brothel business with black magic" is a bit more lofty than current "meanings" in popular literature. For example, after Saltfleet has solved the crime which revealed, in passing, many sordid aspects of the lives of many people, leading one logically to the conclusion that "it's a lousy world" both for victims and killers, Saltfleet at the very end of the story still feels that it is a "good world." He is then informed by a fellow worker that he should have been a clergyman and that he is "wasted in the police force" (211).

Wilson sees an affinity between detecting crimes and saving souls and thus Saltfleet is a new kind of detective, mixing mysticism and science. At one point he even consults a lady who specializes in psychic visions. Not surprisingly, her intuitions prove to be correct. It hardly seems to be playing the game fairly, however, to credit mystic events as equal to so-called real events in a hard-headed detective story. Yet Wilson may have found a new formula as viable for its genre as his new existentialism hopes to be for philosophy.

Colin Wilson as novelist has experimented with the media and genres congenial to his didactic purposes. If he is guilty of insensitive exploitation in the more trivial items, that guilt is a function of the time and place: artists are not supported by institutions such as churches. Free men are free to starve as well as to earn a living by adapting their talents to the market place. If the mature Wilson finds it necessary to sell his wares in a bigger market place, hopefully the buyer will understand. Let the buyer beware, as usual, that he is possibly cause as well as effect, for just as without students there would be no teachers, so without readers there would be no writers. The relationships are symbiotic and thus subject to the fluctuations of all such relationships. The more readers, the more writers needed; and the more writers produced, the more readers needed. But eventually one runs out of readers, leaving the overproduced writers turning out a commodity nobody wants. If Wilson shifts with the winds of opportunity it is because he is authentic enough to relate himself to humanity and its needs. Such awareness is indeed in danger of being mistrusted by skeptics not accustomed to taking a leap of faith to a writer's work in terms of his intentions. This study contends that Wilson's offer as a novelist is essentially honest: "Read my novels, enjoy them if you will, learn from them if you can, and try to trust me." Even Shakespeare asked for no more from his large audiences. The fact that Shakespeare was a greater writer than his audiences needed or often could understand was a dividend for the elite group who received extra pleasure from the performances. Wilson is no Shakespeare, but he has become a competent novelist worthy of being read on his own terms.

CHAPTER 6

The Outsider as Critic-of-All-Trades

WILSON's urgency to communicate can quickly change any genre into a vehicle for his ideas. His critiques of literature, music, sex, poetry, murder, and mysticism; his biographies of Rasputin and Shaw; and his drama on the life of Strindberg — all have advanced his program in one way or another. Sooner or later they show the Colin Wilson trademark as they exhort those who can and will to live more nobly, for Wilson's enthusiasm for the noble permeates all his work. That the existence of nobility must perforce infer the existence of ignobility concerns him little, for Wilson has never inferred that all men can achieve heroic status. In fact, he is quite selective about his nominations for highest significance, particularly among literary figures.

I Existential Criticism

A collection of essays published in 1965, called *Eagle and Earwig*, contains a representative sample of the development of Wilson's critical evaluations of literature. He says that he wrote most of these essays "out of a purely literary interest, as distinguished from a philosophical interest."[1] Nevertheless, these occasional pieces, some of which date back to 1952, often cross lines separating traditional categories. He notes, for example, that the piece "I Glory in the Name of Earwig" (1956) was germinal for *The Stature of Man* (1959), while the essay "Existential Criticism" relates to *The Strength to Dream* (1962). Also, the critical comments on John Cowper Powys and Hemingway predict themes developed in later volumes of the Outsider cycle.

In the essay "I Glory in the Name of Earwig," Wilson reports a panel discussion about the modern theater. The dullness of the discussion, which was enlivened only by an angry altercation between himself and another panelist, set Wilson to pondering. He decided once and for all to opt for heroic eagles who bravely fight for survival rather than for lowly earwigs who never soar above the earth. The image is apt; for, as a critic, Wilson first circles and then zeroes in on the target. "While we wait for the existential hero to come to birth — as he will, slowly and inevitably — we can do no better than continue to spotlight and expose the sources of our chaos. Our business is analysis, unending analysis. Pursued relentlessly and continuously enough, it becomes creation" (54).

He then stresses the distinction between traditional literary criticism and his own existential criticism. The former for him is *merely* literary. The following statement illustrates both the virtues and the vices of Wilson's uncompromising approach to literature:

> The existential critic challenges the author's overall sense of life. No conclusions are accepted separately. The question is not "What do you see?" but "How broad do you see?" Literary criticism assumes that an author is saying to the reader, "I have reached such and such conclusions about life." The existential critic is inclined to retort, "You are not writing about 'life': you are writing about a small section of the world. So before we begin, would you mind telling me exactly what relation you consider that your small section bears to the whole of life?" A writer like Lawrence, Greene, Huxley, or Sartre, implies that his camera lens is far broader than the lens of the reader; that consequently the amount of "life" the reader will find in his novel is far greater than the amount the reader would hope to see with his own unaided eye. The literary critic might be inclined to take this world of the writer at its face value, since his own vision of the world makes no great effort to achieve completeness. But the ideal aim of the existentialist is to summarize life finally, its ultimate affirmations and negations. (68)

Wilson's existential criticism aims wide and deep as it places the object of the analysis in "the context of the writer's life and relation to humanity" (69). In branding as dead the universe of such novelists as Sartre and Robbe-Grillet, Wilson is insisting on the obligation of literature to ask only big questions and to try for only big answers.

In a series of reviewlike essays about writers, famous and obscure, Wilson reveals his own critical concerns during the decade following the publication of *The Outsider* (1956). He asks for reappraisal of such neglected writers as John Cowper Powys, David Lindsay, E. H. Visiak, Imre Madach, L. G. Myers, and Henry Williamson. And for those who suspect Wilson of reactionary political attitudes, his essay on the inadequacies of Ayn Rand is recommended reading, for his verdict is clearly negative, despite passing praise for her story-telling ability and some important insights. Ironically, Wilson's estimate of Ayn Rand's significance approximates what some cautious critics say of Wilson's own work: "It seems to me that Ayn Rand's ideas are such an ingenious mixture of inspired insight and mistaken conclusions that it would be difficult to sort it all out" (219). Wilson adds a postscript detailing Rand's personal discourtesy to him as additional evidence of her wrongness. Apparently existential criticism justifies *ad hominem* comments.

II Music

Wilson's "views" on music are also characteristically irascible. The dust jacket of the American edition of a collection of essays about music whimsically entitled *Chords and Discords* (1966) strikes the controversial keynote: "Not since George Bernard Shaw has there been so free-wheeling and lively an observer of the musical scene — past and present."[2] The blurb writer then predicts that Wilson's "opinions will stir up a storm of critical controversy." Although the controversy has not reached the proportions of a storm, whenever Colin Wilson is involved it is the better part of meteorology to look for unsettled weather.

In these "purely personal opinions on music," Wilson once more probes "the heart of the problem of artistic creation" (97): he insists that a writer or composer must first of all be a great man. Of the Romanticists — Franz Liszt, Richard Wagner, Johannes Brahms, Anton Bruckner, and Gustav Mahler — Wilson surprisingly says that "something went wrong" (47). The coming of the new man had been announced by these composers as surely as the same prophecy had been made by the writers of the time, only to be followed by a reversal. Wilson also accuses Igor Stravinsky and Paul Hindemith of capitulating to a "musical counterpart of logical positivism." Even Schoenberg eventually bogged down as he ignored "existential content" (48).

Trying to shore up his judgments, Wilson reveals his criteria as he surveys the accomplishments of Mozart and Beethoven. Mozart's *The Magic Flute*, for example, "is the real evolutionary article; somehow, it expresses man's most fundamental experience of life and the world" (57). Beethoven's "Ninth," in contrast, relates only to rare moments such as the mass of men seldom know: "Anyone can be courageous when the trumpet sounds and the hair stirs with excitement; it requires something far more godlike to create inner values in Regent Street on a Thursday afternoon. This is something Mozart knew by instinct" (59).

After ranking Beethoven below Mozart, partly because the former's personal life was messy, Wilson plunges into "the problem" of modern music. He convicts Arnold Schoenberg of "life-failure," Anton von Webern of disinterestedness, Hindemith of utilitarianism, and Stravinsky of "deliberately cultivated intellectualism" (75). Because Wilson puts the "whole man" on trial, he is able to acquit only a few of failure. He deplores the fact that so many younger composers have venerated "serialism" as much as writers thirty years ago "gulped down their Joyce, Eliot, and Proust" (83). Greatness is not so easily achieved. "Ultimately," Wilson argues, "the great composer creates what tradition he needs, or manufactures it from odds and ends of other ages" (84).[3] The Outsider with the strength to dream and the courage to act *must* evolve against history and against conditioning.

Citing the "tragedy of Bartok" as a case in point, Wilson notes that Bela Bartok was "conceited, spoilt, and totally self-centered" (90). Without enthusiasm, Wilson adds: "All this is not, of course, to say that Bartok might not be a great composer. Most of the great writers of our century have been highly neurotic — Proust, Joyce, and D. H. Lawrence come to mind" (92); and finally, Wilson decides that Bartok "never became adult" (100).

Wilson's interest in the "two mystics," Alexander Scriabin and Ernest Bloch, is also existential. Observing that Scriabin was regarded in Petersburg before World War I "as a kind of artistic Rasputin," Wilson yields to his admiration for people who break through barriers. Because Scriabin was an Outsider, a "creature" who needs "freedom as urgently as he needs air" (107), Wilson prefers him to Frederick Chopin. Labeling Bloch "a Jewish romantic," Wilson finds that paradoxically most of Bloch's music sounds English. All in all, however, Wilson decides that "Bloch is not a great composer" (111).

After disposing of these serious composers, Wilson chats about popular music. He admits his inability to "connect as human beings" with such jazz men as Coleman Hawkins, Roy Eldridge, Thad Jones, and Cannonball Adderley and to find pleasurable excitement in listening to their performances. The admission signifies that he has not yet been able to evaluate them existentially. Although jazz as a myth of vitality interests Wilson, the "semi-intellectual developments" of such composer-performers as Dave Brubeck and Lennie Tristano seem to him too narrow.

As for English music, Wilson does not easily spot a truly great composer, although he ranks Sir Edward Elgar as the best. Many minor composers are dutifully named before Wilson casts his existential eye upon Vaughan Williams, John Ireland, Arnold Bax, Arthur Bliss, William Walton, and Benjamin Britten; but even these do not quite measure up to his standards. After some not very relevant notes upon opera, Wilson comments on American music in a final chapter. Observing that America has not yet created a unique culture of its own, Wilson concludes that most American composers "fail to impress as *creative* individuals" (195). Charles Ives and Elliott Carter are exceptions, for they possess more personal integrity. Clearly all music for Wilson is a means of getting to know the composer as a person who is good or bad to the extent that he *honestly* goes about his business.

Wilson's opinions about music and composers were at first understood more clearly by reviewers than were either his philosophical essays or novels — at least at the level of musical criticism. Wilson's insistence, however, that even brilliant composers must also be good men was less generally acceptable. One reviewer praised Wilson's "lively and individual approach," noting that the book was "stuffed with startling and enthusiastic judgments."[4] To the extent that the reader agreed with Wilson's judgments he was likely to consider the work "exceptionally healthy."[5] The rejection of Wilson's thesis that a composer is not a great man unless he has done more than compose fine music is really a rejection of Wilson's new existentialism, however, and as such involves more than what one critic was willing to admit. Consequently Wilson was again called "callow" and "immature."[6]

III *Murder*

In addition to his exploitation of murder in his novels,[7] Wilson has systematically studied the lives of famous "real" murderers. The first of his projects, reported on in collaboration with Patricia Pitman, resulted in a collection of brief biographies of several hundred killers entitled *Encyclopaedia of Murder* (1961).[8] The work was prefaced with an essay by Wilson, "The Study of Murder," which delineates his philosophical interest in homicide. Convinced that all art aims at intensifying consciousness, Wilson regards murder as a kind of negative art that illustrates some men's fervent attempts to escape tedium and triviality. Defending his special interest in depicting violence, Wilson distinguishes between the vivid description of the act and the act itself. For him, the description is more significant; for it "creates a resistance in the reader; when the cause of this resistance is analyzed, the result is an insight into positive values" (23 - 24).

The cases cited in the 1961 volume do not always fulfill Wilson's premises. It is clear enough that murderers experience some kind of negative confrontation with life and its values and that the compiler was adequate to respond to the cases, which became for *him* stimuli expanding his own awareness. But browsing through an encyclopaedia in which killers are listed alphabetically is not so vivid an experience as living among murderers or as reading coherent and expanded biographies. Understandably, as Patricia Pitman indicates in her part of the preface, this work cannot pretend to be comprehensive: "During the last hour or two more murders will have been committed in Mexico alone" (49). Critical responses to the work fluctuated between the polarities of "engrossing" and "depressing." It was also called "macabre in a Madame Tussaud kind of way."[9] It was found useful by criminologists and crime-story writers, but it never attracted the attention Wilson had hoped for it.

Later Wilson reworked some of the same material and also added new killers in *A Casebook of Murder* (1969).[10] Subtitled "A Compelling Study of the World's Most Macabre Murder Cases," this work is more unified and more readable than the earlier one. Although Wilson announces the theme of the book as "the sociology of murder — the changing patterns of murder in Western Society," he also says that he regards murder as "a response to a certain problem of human freedom: not as a social problem, or a psychological problem, or even a moral problem . . . but as an *existential* problem in the sense that the word would be used by Sartre or Heidegger" (21).

Philosophical interest in murder does not necessarily make for clear definitions of the moral categories involved. Any "ordinary" person understandably hesitates to murder as a creative act. *A Casebook of Murder*, however, peers into the darkness of murder for light on the human condition. Although Wilson would agree for social reasons with the need to restrain killers from their artistic performances, he resists condemning the creative killer's impulse.

There are, of course, other ways of viewing murder, such as the points of view of the victim or of the law. Wilson, solemnly supporting a positive existentialism grounded in intuitions of freedom, looks for all and any evidence that men can will themselves to act, even if the act is murder. When the time is out of joint and the *Lebensraum* is too confining, what can a poor Outsider do but complain, sulk, philosophize, or kill? Wilson's interest in murder also emphasizes method, for *A Casebook* is an attempt "to sketch an overall picture of the patterns of murder in various centuries, particularly the seventeenth, eighteenth, nineteenth and twentieth . . ." (23). Certain "cases," however, did not qualify for inclusion. For example, assassination is omitted from this discussion as being qualitatively different from murder in that it is usually related to political or moral commitments rather than being a response to boredom or a triumph over frustration.

When almost every crime was a capital offense, the criminal always expected the worst punishment even for slight delinquencies; therefore, he might as well kill. The having-nothing-to-lose psychology of the underprivileged, who are often also the overpunished, encourages violence. Wilson notes, almost with relish, the history of attempts to make the death penalty something more horrible than simple execution. He seems to enjoy describing tortures of the living and imaginative debasements of the dead, but he fully understands that the punishers can be more wanton than the original criminals.

Not a few civilized people share Wilson's interest in murder, for crime stories are perennial favorites among cultivated readers. Although Wilson's book, like any compendium, may disappoint, by certain omissions, those who have their own favorites among famous criminals, his is a serious attempt to gather together enough information to hazard some conclusions about changing patterns of homicide throughout the years. Phoebe Adams, an astute critic, summarized the weaknesses and strengths of the book neatly when she wrote that "Wilson does not get far with his thesis that patterns of homicide have changed in the last century, partly because information for earlier centuries is scattered and not always dependable, and partly because he is having so much fun rehashing gaudy cases. The bloody minded reader will have fun too."[11]

Recently Wilson has published a third study of murder. In *Order of Assassins* (1972),[12] he speculates about the psychology of murder and theoretically connects the characteristics of his 1956 Outsider with a special type of killer. The Outsider, defined at great length but necessarily not always sharply delineated in earlier works, is now regarded by Wilson as a potential assassin. Frustrated but talented outcasts may release energy in violent acts instead of in creative ones. As failed artists, they become more frustrated and then more violent as they assert their wills and break through barriers. But, instead of writing poems or painting pictures, they kill. A London reviewer, after noting that "the main impression left by the writing is one of 'library psychology,' " was fair enough to perceive Wilson's objective and to credit him with it, namely, "a genuine effort to understand a sinister symptom of social disease. . . ."[13] All in all, however, Wilson's so-called crime novels explore the subject more compellingly.

IV *Biography*

Wilson's interests sometimes appear to range too far afield for him ever to return to his original objective of creating and promoting a new philosophy. His concerns, however, seldom shoot off on an irretrievable tangent, for he keeps his goal well in sight no matter what he is working on. Wilson's version of the life of Rasputin, called *Rasputin and the Fall of the Romanovs,*[14] is an investigation of madness and its coordinates rather than a true biography; for the youthful philosopher was eager to define the *real* Rasputin as one of his own Outsiders. Instead of cataloging facts, Wilson presents Rasputin as an Outsider constantly trying to realize himself in his progress from servant-priest to patron of the Tsar. The author carefully indicates — as *he* sees them — the dimensions of Rasputin's greatness, the depths of his psychic powers, and his capacities for suffering. He finds in the monk the same kind of greatness that infused Nijinsky's dancing and Nietzsche's visions. Rasputin had "crystallized" his essence into a formidable destiny. For Wilson, Rasputin's greatness could not be contaminated by ordinary infections: "Like Nietzsche, he was born free of the diseases of his time. He had the natural crude health and self-belief that characterizes so many men of genius born out of the 'people' " (213). Although Wilson succeeds only partially in establishing Rasputin as a potentiated Outsider, he is more successful with his next choice of subject for a life portrait.

Most of the reviewers of *Rasputin* ironically took the wrong kind of delight in it. One critic was pleased by the way Wilson "gaily demolished" his biography-writing predecessors.[15] Another asserted that "The sheer cockiness of Mr. Wilson is entertaining."[16] In general, however, serious historians may well neglect Wilson's biographies as much too biased. Wilson is adverse to researching a subject for the sake of research alone. He has been deeply interested in all the subjects of his writing, and that interest shows up in his emphases and proportions. No harm is done, however, for it is to Wilson's credit that he seldom pretends to scholarly definitiveness.

That Wilson would write a biography of his one real hero, George Bernard Shaw, was inevitable. As a lad, Wilson had appointed himself Shaw's successor, and his admiration for the Irish genius has never faltered. Feeling as he does that "the Shavian torch" has been entrusted to him, Wilson's study of his master, *Bernard Shaw: A Reassessment* (1969)[17] is permeated with his enthusiasms, some of which result in special pleas. For example, he rejects the currently fashionable discounting of Shaw as a late Victorian. Instead, he sees the irascible dramatist as a prophetic philosopher, one whose best works predict the optimistic existentialism which Wilson has been promoting. "Shaw's evolutionary vision," he concludes, "was a kind of dawn in which new things become visible in the half-light. Since then, the light has grown stronger, and it becomes possible to see an answer to the question: What shall we *do*?" (294).

Although, in all fairness, Wilson does admit that existential psychologists such as Frankl and Maslow would never consider themselves Shavian evolutionists, he does insist, as he characteristically confounds faith and fact, that Shaw was the "original prophet" of the existential revolution. Shaw, himself, of course, had announced that he was the most advanced man of his time; for he sincerely felt that he had solved all the important problems of his day despite the fact that no one had really listened. Also, Shaw had persistently struggled for success: he had written many unpublished novels before hitting the public fancy first as a critic and then as a dramatist. Like Wilson, he finally appreciated the irony of being praised not for the ideas he valued but for his more superficial qualities, such as his verbal dexterity. Although Wilson's fame came more quickly than he had really expected, it was still the bitterest fame of that time; therefore, Wilson's interest in Shaw is strengthened by his personal identification with the man. As Shaw's self-appointed successor, Wilson undertook to expedite the breakthrough which his master had predicted was possible but which he had not completely accomplished himself.

Shaw estimated that 5 percent of humanity dominated the other 95 percent. He asserted that among the dominant minority there were "higher evolutionary types" capable of *willing* a leap forward; and Wilson counts himself, of course, among this superior minority. Shaw also never doubted that he was different from the mass of men. Although his conviction made him seem immodest, he knew that dullards prefer their own kind to immodest geniuses. Wilson has been extending the Shavian quest for brightness into a philosophical search for an existentialism beyond nihilistic despair. As he traces the course of Shaw's career, he emphasizes the dramatist's "ideas"; for, like Shaw, Wilson also suffered from critics who either could not or would not try to understand his *thinking*.

Sympathetic with the persona which Shaw took such pains to create, Wilson classifies Shaw as a Romantic who artfully made his plays "acceptable to the intellectually fastidious by a certain stripping away of sentimentalism" (xii). He also attributes to Shaw the invention of the "alienation effect" which Brecht later popularized. Shaw in his dramas did not pretend to mirror reality. In fact, he carefully released his audiences from the need to "believe" in his characters and their eccentric behavior. Shavian wit is all the more delightful because it is incredible.

Shaw's rejection of Naturalism and scientific reductionism makes him, for Wilson, a visionary. Although his plays are not all aesthetically good, they are "all about the same theme: the obscure creative drive of the 'Life Force,' and the way that it makes people do things they find difficult to understand in terms of everyday logic" (166). Wilson believes that even Shaw's most fumbling creations are redeemed by the writer's spirit, but some of the devices which Shaw used to safeguard that spirit have helped build a legend which now obscures the *real* man. As an existential critic, Wilson tries to penetrate the legend; and he "reassesses," therefore, those aspects of Shaw's work which confirm his own confidence in a new existentialism. Wilson ranks Shaw on the side of the angels, and it certainly never occurs to Wilson that he is himself also not clearly on the same side.

Opinion about Wilson's treatment of Shaw has been divided. It is self-evident that the work is not scholarly. After the scholars had noted that fact, at least one praised the book as "a provocative study worthy of attention" while warning the reader "that more is to be learned in it about Colin Wilson than about Bernard Shaw."[18] It is true that Wilson uses Shaw's life partly to promote his own philosophy — and naturally the usual objections were made to such exploitation — but he also obviously worships his subject. One critic observed that the fact that "Shaw survives such zealotry is convincing evidence of the vitality of his plays and prose." Of the "reassessments" which Wilson hoped would support his claims about Shaw's significance, the same critic decided that they ranged from preposterous to persuasive."[19] Not surprisingly, Wilson was even praised for *not* having handled the subject in a scholarly fashion. Typically, the worst that he could be called was "an informed, vital, opinionated Shaw enthusiast."[20] Reaction to Wilson's work by the end of the sixties often make both a virtue and a vice out of his intensity. Such ambivalent verdicts, however, are not really miscarriages of justice in the case of Wilson, for the frequency with which Wilson's words are often simultaneously rejected and praised probes the heart of the matter. Putative prophets arouse anxiety in those accustomed to less passion. Colin Wilson offers no comfortable compromises. He believes in himself and asks others to believe in him also.

V *Drama*

Wilson's early failure as a dramatist began when his first play was rejected by the Royal Court Theatre soon after the flash success of *The Outsider*. Wilson has revived from time to time his interest in writing plays, but not many have shared the playwright's enthusiasm for his own work, therefore it is not surprising that his best experiment in using the drama to promote his message reads well as a closet drama — in the quite respectable tradition of Goethe's *Faust*. Wilson's *Strindberg* appeared in 1970 and was published in England by Calder and Boyars as "Playscript 31" of a series of avant-garde plays. The series includes experimentalists such as Antonin Artaud, Nathalie Sarraute, and Pablo Picasso. Wilson's pleasure in being included in this distinguished company is defensible, and it may be that his earnest dramatic projections may yet be recognized as something more than vehicles for ideas. Such devices as extremely long speeches in which characters say what Wilson has selected for them to say without regard for the audience's need to be stimulated as well as informed are not dramatically effective. In the context of Wilson's existential objective, however, the *mind* of a character is for him most important; and Strindberg's mind obviously interested Wilson personally as an example of the psychopathology of genius. Wilson's use of mind-revealing soliloquies is, nevertheless, tedious despite such stage-business as fading spotlights and fantastic costumes aimed at establishing a mystical ambience.

Strindberg is avowedly subjective; no attempt is made to tell an evolving story about Strindberg. Instead, Wilson has tried to project the characteristics of Strindberg's mind and soul. Using many of Strindberg's own words, he hoped virtually to materialize this mystical rationalist. The play opens upon a "set" identified as "the room of Strindberg's flat in the Blue Tower, 85 Drotninggaten,

Stockholm." Although the room is presumably illuminated only by the moon, two figures can be seen in bed. Presently one of the figures, Strindberg obviously, gets up. He is described as sixty years old, with a leonine head and "the face [is] a little haggard, the eyes tense and haunted — a man who never relaxes completely" (7). Strindberg soon begins to talk, and he pauses in the course of the drama only briefly now and then to allow a few subsidiary characters to question him or to confront him with a refutation. An aged, sick man, whose pleasure in self-flagellation was underlined by his awareness of evils beyond his control, Strindberg, as Wilson projects him, is a complex personality. Using Strindberg's physician, Dr. Steinmetz, as a prop with whom the dramatist has both imaginary and real conversations, Wilson explores the dimensions of paranoia and supersanity.

After Strindberg has summarized the main facts of his romantic life, he announces that "it is the nature of a woman to destroy men, just as it's the nature of caterpillars to destroy cabbages" (12). When Dr. Steinmetz suggests that this view is "rather . . . exaggerated" (13), Strindberg appeals to the fact that all his women have betrayed him. In passing, Strindberg also notes his affinity with Nietzsche, another man destroyed by a woman. Then he suddenly shifts emphasis and denies that women destroy men. Instead, he blames "the forces behind history" which "want to destroy us. Or perhaps only to tear our souls apart, to flay us into strength. And they've selected the women as their scorpions — to sting us, to whip us, to lacerate the flesh and the soul" (32).

In the climactic scene of the play, which takes place in Strindberg's mind as he sleeps, Strindberg is on trial for libeling and defaming members of the community in his works. Dr. Steinmetz, called upon to evaluate Strindberg's sanity, proposes a Freudian explanation of the writer's eccentricities. Insecure as a child, Strindberg had been trapped in a vicious circle. The more hostility he aroused in others, the more anxious he became and the more hostility he stimulated. Strindberg claims, however, that he possesses strange powers, such as the ability to kill people simply by wishing them dead. In a long monologue which contains an undiluted Wilsonian message, Strindberg analyzes his "instinct" for life which transcends reason and logic. Exalting intuition, Strindberg cites Swedenborg's "devastations" as similar to his own experiences — a seeming illness which is really "a disciplinary force," the purpose of which is "to bring man to the threshold of a new stage in his evolution" (68). Strindberg predicts the coming of "a new era in which there will be a strange awakening" (69). Like all Outsiders, Strindberg had tried to "scale the plains of heaven." Although he had failed, his suffering has redeemed him.

When Strindberg asks the judge to pass sentence on him, the judge tells him that there has been no trial. With the help of his faithful but misunderstood wife, Strindberg finally realizes that he had put himself on trial, found himself guilty, and sentenced himself to death. "That's the logical conclusion of a lifelong defect," he announces (76). Shouting that this "will to death" must be "torn out," Strindberg moves out of his dream into the body which has never really risen from the bed. The dramatist, "who wanted a goddess" for his woman but was himself "afraid to be a god," was a true Outsider, stranded all his life between the obtainable and the unobtainable.

Unlike those philosophers who have become silent about certain mysteries, Wilson tries to articulate ineffables. *Strindberg* is a worthy effort to delineate one man's passionate attempts to rise above the zero of ordinary living. Strindberg failed as a man, but his dramas for Wilson honor all who "want to smash and rage and tear until they've destroyed the worm of triviality that turns the heart into a rotten apple" (69).

VI *Mysticism*

Apologies for poetry, both in the narrow sense of acknowledging guilt for being a poet and in the deep sense of defending poetry, are numerous and varied. From Sir Philip Sidney's famous defense to T. S. Eliot's solemn explications, a long line of essays exists which investigate the magic of verbal incantations and analyze the visionary nature of poets. Colin Wilson seeks in poetry a liberating experience similar to the visions of mystics. A man who intends to live virtually forever and who sees himself as only beginning his voyage into creativity after writing more than thirty books is necessarily impatient with anything less than vitalizing experiences. Wilson's interest in poetry is thus less literary than philosophical, and it is also really less philosophical than religious.

Wilson tells how, in the late 1960s, while drinking beer one day with Lawrence Ferlinghetti in San Francisco, he and the poet began to discuss "the nature of the mystical experience." When Ferlinghetti asked Wilson to write an essay on the subject, the result was a short book (published by Ferlinghetti's City Lights Press) entitled *Poetry and Mysticism* (1969). Later, an expanded version on the same subject was published in London by Hutchinson (1970).[21] Wilson's so-called mystical experience differs from that of traditional religionists as well as latter-day experimenters with drug-induced visions in that his "faith" has been underwritten by evidence he believes scientifically sound. He has, for example, endorsed "the scientific pursuit of the psychological mechanisms of the 'intensity experience.' " "I am convinced," he says in the opening paragraph of *Poetry and Mysticism*, "that at some point in his evolution, man will achieve complete control over those floodgates of inner-energy that create the mystical experience. I also believe that he will do this by a *learning process*, exactly as he might learn to play Beethoven sonatas or drive a helicopter" (11).

Such a prediction, based on observation as well as on stubborn hope, has little to do with the Christian doctrine of salvation. Wilson is at once both too radical for theologians who witness to God's grace and too mystical for behavioral scientists who report the absence of ineffables in the laboratory. When Wilson defines poetry as "the sudden feeling that everything is good" and defends poetry as a means to expand consciousness, his seemingly careless mixture of enthusiasm alienates him from more rigid partisans. His determination to encourage men to stretch their minds beyond immediacy includes, however, cautions against the use of magic tricks or addictive drugs as substitutes for the pure experience. For Wilson, the poetic and the mystical experiences are identical and are neither substitutes nor stimulants for one another.

In the longer version of the essay, *Poetry and Mysticism*, Wilson exemplifies his ideas by referring to the works of William Butler Yeats, Rupert Brooke, A. L. Rouse, and Nikos Kazantzakis. This rather improbable foursome — as Wilson manipulates the data — yield a common factor: "the feeling they convey of the ultimate *frustration of the poet's aim*" (213). At first, Wilson seems to be defeating himself by admitting the existence of so much frustration; but he soon reaches the positive goal he is seeking. "*Man must learn*," he announces excitedly, "*to destroy the element of negation in his own consciousness*" (221). Brooke had momentarily achieved the goal in his "sudden forgetfulness of personality" (110). But Brooke died too soon to potentiate his talent. And even Yeats, despite his visionary intensity, becomes for Wilson "a bad poet in the sense in which the word is generally understood" (158). Only Rouse and Kazantzakis succeeded in escaping despair in "sudden total absorption in beauty" (183).

Poetry and Mysticism, even in the longer version, does not pretend to be a definitive critical work, and the *Times* unfairly gave the book very short shrift: "Mr. Wilson's ability to come up with answers as remarkable as his questions is one of the — very minor — wonders of the world."[22] Wilson, however, had not hoped to become even a minor wonder. The work is a declaration of intent, a promise to research into the heart of a mystery which may prove to be less mysterious than underexplored. Therefore, the result of Wilson's continuing curiosity about such mysteries, as is always the case with a Wilsonian interest, is another and bigger book — a compendium of occult lore. Wilson's interest in occultism is a logical extension of his conviction that at least 5 percent of human beings are capable of achieving a superconsciousness not yet fully potentiated. For years, he has been collecting bits of evidence to support his thesis, and, as a result, *The Occult* (1972)[23] is a compendium of mystic lore which adds up to a survey qua defense. Like one trying to justify an unusual religious conversion, Wilson cites compatible testimonials from others; and the result is a mixture of allusions, quotations, arguments, and "facts."

Each of the three sections of the work fulfills its promise rather more than less. Part one is a survey of occultism; part two, a quick history of magic; part three, a catchall for those topics not adequately covered in the first two sections, such as "witchcraft, lycanthropy, and vampirism, the history of spiritualism, the problem of ghosts and poltergeists" (31 - 32). In the final chapter, "Glimpses," Wilson summarizes the metaphysical implications of the topic.

Wilson's attitude toward the occult changed during his research of his subject. Although his grandmother was a spiritualist, Wilson asserts that he had formerly been unimpressed by both spiritualism and occultism. He had felt that "there was something *trivial* about all this preoccupation with life after death, as there is about chess or ballroom dancing" (32 - 33). After probing the subject more deeply, however, Wilson was convinced by the consistency of the evidence pointing to the high probability of life after death, out-of-the-body astral projection, and reincarnation.

Characteristically, Wilson sees no serious contradictions between his insistence that "the reality of life after death has been established beyond all reasonable doubt" and his statement that he still sympathizes, nevertheless, "with the philosophers and scientists who regard it as emotional nonsense, because I am temperamentally on their side" (33). At the same time he accuses the same scientists of "closing their eyes to evidence that would convince them if it concerned the mating habits of albino rats or the behavior of alpha particles" (33).

Wilson has hoped to extend credibility without embracing credulousness. Such a fine distinction is attractive to Wilson but it is delicately nuanced. Most critical opinions of the work conceded that, despite many omissions, *The Occult* does make interesting reading. A journal professing to evaluate books as good or bad buys for libraries called the work "especially valuable for the thinking reader who is searching for a book on the occult that is more than a collection of marvels, absurdities, or 'do-it-yourself' techniques."[24] The *Times* reviewer, as usual, was less enthusiastic: "Most of the massive volume is a hotchpotch of magic, witchcraft, spiritualism, and the like . . . Mr. Wilson should stick to fiction. . . ."[25]

Joyce Carol Oates praised the work as a "book of wonders" and recommended it highly as "one of those rich, strange, perplexing, infinitely surprising works that repay many readings. Though it contains a great deal of history it is really, like most of Colin Wilson's books, about the future."[26] Indeed, the work does look to the future also for its ultimate validation, although Wilson has been cautious in assuming the truth of all the evidence he quotes, summarizes, and discusses. As if he were disdaining the paradox which looms when one tries to predict events which by definition are unpredictable, such as miracles and other paranormal happenings, Wilson emerges as one of the first of the intellectuals interested in the validity of paraintellectual events such as hunches and premonitions. In fact, Wilson presents his case and the case for the occult *scientifically;* that is, he is determined to *prove* that occult phenomena do occur. Yet he must know that "proving" is by no means a certain method of establishing the realness of anything, for "proof" is a statistical concept dependent upon an arbitrary number of witnesses testifying that the event in question did happen and that they *saw* it, *heard* it, *felt* it, and *smelled* it themselves. How many witnesses it takes to establish validity and reliability is still moot. In a sense, Wilson may be overextending his enthusiasm for truth and eventually find himself impacted by more than one paradox. Many of his ideas emerge as contrary to received opinion, and some of his hostile critics have pointed out that he also contradicts himself here and there. A paradox, of course, is a statement that contradicts itself as it tells the truth or as it lies or as it does both simultaneously. At this place and in this time paradoxes are quite respectable, and any man who claims to be a liar, for example, is credited with telling the truth, while most men who claim to tell the truth are assumed to be liars.

VII *Critic of All Trades: The Paradox*

Colin Wilson's thirst for more and more knowledge must perforce always outrun his research just as his productivity must lag behind his research. That he never will have time enough to report all the results of the time he has already spent in pursuing knowledge is self-evident if one includes the reporting of the reporting he is currently doing. Such a paradox does not overwhelm Wilson as it might ordinary mortals; yet it looms now and then as a threat to his professional status. Eager to reach wider and wider readerships, Wilson has begun to popularize some of his ideas for special groups, such as teenagers. In 1966 he reduced and slanted some of his ideas about sexual impulses and their relationships to man's imagination as presented originally in the fifth volume of his Outsider cycle, *Origins of the Sexual Impulse* (1963), and gathered them together in a little volume called *Sex and the Intelligent Teenager.*[27] Therein he makes it clear to his young readers that he is championing their rights to explore the subject themselves, that he himself takes great joy in sex, and that they are bright enough, he assumes, to make decisions for themselves once given the facts about the power and value of sexuality. He assures his "bright" readers that "of all human experiences, sex gives man the clearest sense of freedom" (191). He defines the reflexive nature of human sexuality, insisting, for example, that the orgasm is a willful and imaginative part of the act. He stresses the uses of sex in achieving not only freedom but the power to act creatively in other ways. In his enthusiasm he predicts that today's enlightened youth "will discover that he can change the world" (192).

It is significant that Wilson addressed the work to the *intelligent* teenager. In so doing he begs one of the big questions: could the proper use of sex make *all* youths bright? He tells his readers that they are bright by definition in that youth is positively correlated with intelligence; yet he must assume that there are duller readers who would abuse his message, distorting it into a license to indulge in antisocial behavior.

Wilson is typically eager to get the new world underway and thus is seldom hesitant to tackle a big subject with the tools and the facts he has on hand. He is a liberated Outsider himself and as such assumes the possibility of other Outsiders becoming equally liberated. Yet as a critic and as a reformer he could discover that his own liberation alienates him from the as-yet-enslaved whom he wants to free. He is impatient with the neuroses of those who have not found the vitality he urges them to search for; yet he knows that their apathy is not really an impenetrable barrier. If it were, there would be no sense in trying to reach them, and Wilson is always determined to make eminent sense. He *intends* to make sense, and he credits intention with the power to achieve that goal. In urging others to do likewise, that is, to *intend* to throw off despair and other debilitating emotions, he faces a paradox, for some of his readers do not want to throw off despair and, because Wilson himself has glorified their "will," they are reinforced for asserting their will *against* him!

The final paradox that Wilson now confronts, it seems to the author of this study, is that what began as his major asset could become a liability. Wilson early discovered how different he was from most people. He knew he was himself an Outsider, and as he researched the subject he began to see how Outsiders could courageously resist defeat. He has succeeded so well in his program that he is becoming less and less an Outsider himself. Will he lose touch eventually with those very readers he is determined to enlighten, many of whom are forlorn youths who greatly admire his writings and who are impressionable enough to want to model their tastes and interests after Wilson's? The answer is an optimistic "probably not," for, although Wilson is now beyond his original outsiderism, he is still idiomatically an Outsider insofar as his professionalism substitutes deliberate control over his writing in place of the original passion and enthusiasm. As he becomes increasingly aware that there is not time enough — even for him — to do everything and to be everything, he has tempered impatience with a touch of resignation, that first hint of autumn and the end of the happy summer of youth. Wilson is finally less and less a critic-of-all-trades and more and more a professional adult responding to certain realities like most other grown-ups. He has not capitulated to the paradox that one loses one's life in living. Instead he has learned from it that one also gains a firmer hold on reality as time passes.

CHAPTER 7

The Outsider as New Existentialist: An Evaluation

PRESENTING himself as a prophet of reality, Wilson has always believed that his work has the highest kind of significance. Although he may be wrong, his confidence is usually more reassuring than the demure modesty of more timid candidates for significance. Wilson has boldly faulted philosophy for having snubbed the occult sciences and humanistic psychology. Philosophy has had serious trouble lately deciding just what kind of reality it is dealing with, for reasoning itself is now rationally suspected of no longer being reasonable! Paradoxes clutter the scene, and Wilson has accepted the challenge to attempt to outface some of them. In his championing of human freedom, Wilson is inimical both to behaviorism and to pessimistic existentialism. His rejection of conventional formulas which purport to soften disagreements between thinkers and experimenters differentiates his position from those who have pledged allegiance to one school or another. Because Colin Wilson believes he alone is right, to try him in any one partisan court inevitably miscarries. As a mystic who has not forsaken rationalism, and as an optimist who has not turned his back on reality, he has been forced to design a *new* existentialism that incorporates the insights of contemporary phenomenology and humanistic psychology. It is not possible to evaluate what Wilson has been trying to do without some knowledge of these two important areas.

Most attempts to define phenomenology begin with origins that tie the "movement" to the reaction against British Empiricism led by Franz Brentano and Edmund Husserl at the end of the nineteenth century.[1] Husserl in turn had been influenced by William James, who was himself highly eclectic. Thus a respectable background of truth-seeking supports the tradition which has sought to be even more disciplined and rigorous than the physical and biological sciences. It is clear, however, that "disciplined" and "rigorous" are conscience-easing words; for, unless they are defined in terms of procedures, they are likely to deteriorate into empty verbalizations. The assumption remains, nevertheless, that reality *can* be perceived if one digs deeply enough and keeps checking against biases, including those of the checker.

Husserl is credited by his supporters with inaugurating explorations into a reality that is not arbitrarily limited by a methodological bias. One impassioned defender proudly proclaims that "there is a vast range of facts and patterns which are open to the new philosophical discipline of phenomenology."[2] Presumably earlier disciplines had failed to find all the facts and all the patterns. Wilson's *new* existentialism also emerges as a protest against the inadequacy of earlier science. He is urgent, because he is convinced that mere science is not just modestly inadequate but arrogantly so in its assumption of having the exclusive road to truth. When behavioral scientists emptied the organism of mental content, they did so because for them only observables can be manipulated. They contended that "thought" may only be inferred from overt behavior; thus the "mind" to them as such is not *really* real. Behaviorists prefer to observe the relationships between what the experimenter does and what the subject does as a result of what the experimenter (or a change in the environment) does. Then they test the generalization induced from their observations; and, if the test is passed, they have for the time being a *fact* about human behavior. Such a fact, of course, seems trivial to philosophers who are in pursuit of moral imperatives. But, when the behaviorist measures thirst in units of water deprivation, he does not have to ask the subject if he *feels* thirsty, nor does he evaluate the subject's good faith; therefore, he avoids subjective fallacies at the price of ethical indifference. Because such operational definitions rule out consciousness, the creative philosopher accuses the scientist of debasing human nature and calls him a reductionist.

As man is categorized as a mere organism in order for scientists to handle him, the champions of the spirit have tried to restore human dignity by reasserting man's complexity, particularly his will and the moral correlatives of freedom. Once again they hold man responsible for choosing to exist, and a few even accuse the sick of choosing to be sick and the dead of choosing to die. Introspection regains a respectable status, and life goals are repristinated in idealistic terms as terror and anxiety emerge as neither God's will nor the human condition. The twice-born man knows that he has earned his own happiness, has willed his own salvation.

Colin Wilson has addressed himself to strictly contemporary problems as he tries to penetrate the fog that for him obscures *real* reality. His methodology participates in his urgency, for his creed specifies that man is always more than any method. At times, Wilson may be only absurdly heroic, in the sense of working against overwhelming odds; but he knows it more often than not and indulges in a minimum of despair and irony. Indeed, his urgency usually eradicates irony and discourages witty trivia as he fights the slackness which would follow his acceptance of despair as terminal. Determined to survive, he feels that, as the first new existentialist, he has earned the right to his optimism. Anyway, the fact of his ultimate wrongness or rightness may be insignificant when compared with the possible significance of his thrust and impact in nontechnical contexts.

Intentionality, the phenomenologist insists, is what counts. An honest philosopher is not supposed to reject an old method because of boredom or to embrace a new method because it seems more interesting. As the new existentialism takes over phenomenological goals and methods, it is committed to studying all phenomena at the risk of losing its way in order to find it. Not surprisingly, Wilson's earnest rejection of nihilistic positions, insofar as he can detect them, implies religious values. *Patently,* life contains Absurdity. As Wilson rejects the inexorableness of Absurdity — that is, that irresoluble discrepancy between what is and what might have been — he is rejecting certain evidence; that is, he is refuting the validity of the claim that life is absurd. Yet because he has been trained to respect all evidence, even when it contradicts his own hopes, he must rise to the occasion heroically. Thus he sees himself as alone and unafraid in a world he himself is remaking.

Uneasiness in the face of heroics is the mark today of the well-adjusted man. That uneasiness combined with sober evaluations of technical matters such as careless documentation (Wilson admits that he is by nature untidy) has motivated "bad" reviews by "good" critics of many items in the Wilson canon. The ranking of Wilson by more narrowly committed philosophers as a charlatan is ofen a function of placing him in the wrong category; for, as a hero, Wilson is a bad philosopher only in passing. The big vision projected by Wilson is a promised land, not a map of a familiar country. Such envisioning is accepted by the mass of nondreamers as healthy only in moderation; excessive indulgence is considered dangerous, even insane. The fear of schizophrenia is the hobgoblin of little minds who make the contemporary scene into an athletic field rather than a battleground. Wilson can be quixotic; he is sometimes brash and impudent; but he is never afraid.

It is important to understand that Wilson's philosophy, which is avowedly now something other than traditional existentialism or science, may eventually become scientific in the complete meaning of the noun-become-adjective. At present, he makes no claim to systematic completeness; but he is far from willing to renounce the possibility of knowing all about knowing, and so he has opted for extending the techniques of finding out and for liberalizing the modality of knowing per se by exalting intuition, vastations, and peak experiences as valid modes of "prehension" leading to meaning-perception. Balanced, then, at the edge of mysticism in a universe which is obviously not governed by any of the old Sunday-School gods, Wilson asks as earnestly as Julian Huxley has for religion without revelation. He would also develop a science without limitations on freedom. He urges man toward salvation by exhorting and stimulating him to see more, to hear more, to feel more, to touch more — that is, to apprehend what is *really* out there and what is *really* inside oneself. The Outsider is invited to embrace the complete universe and to cure his outsiderism.

I Introduction to the New Existentialism

As supplement to the six volumes of his Outsider cycle, Wilson in 1966 summarized in *Introduction to the New Existentialism* (1966)[3] his "position" at that time. The work is a readable and an informative guide through these complex areas. Using the terms "new existentialism" and "phenomenological existentialism" interchangeably — and without capitalizing the term — Wilson outlines the case for his claim of having broken out of the dead end of the old, pessimistic existentialism. Although most of his arguments are familiar to those who know the earlier essays and several novels, this volume is unusually lucid; for Wilson clearly reveals in it his first interest in those existential psychologists who have utilized the findings and conjectures of phenomenology in effecting therapies that seem to work.

Again and again Wilson objects strenuously to accepting an empty and meaningless universe. Stressing the evidence that consciousness is intentional, Wilson resists Sartre's gloomy conclusion that such intentionality is only apparent and thus bad faith. Wilson enthusiastically endorses Husserl's attack on distorted perceptions of oneself and of others. The ultimate for Wilson is an increase in self-knowledge that leads not to sadness and frustration but to control over one's own existence and increased understanding of others. Supporting concepts, such as an innate need to know and an innate capacity for "meaning perception" in contrast to "immediacy perception," reinforce Wilson's argument. Wilson is intent on opening the door that Sartre marked "no exit."

II *The One Percent That Counts*

In a crucial essay, "Existential Psychology: A Novelist's Approach,"[4] Wilson explores the metaphor of a debilitating robot in man. He has discovered in himself, he asserts, a mechanical kind of awareness which has become a surrogate for more creative kinds of awareness. He deplores man's capacity for developing such internalized automated systems. Recommending a careful examination of this robot-like mechanism, Wilson estimates that presently consciousness is 99 percent mechanical. He then hits his target: "But it is that other one percent that counts. That one percent, by continuous effort, can gradually subdue the other 99 percent."[5] The desired objective, of course, is to actualize the "real me" which is "pure freedom." This quintessential freedom is found only in certain intense experiences, such as the sexual orgasm. Such relatively pure consciousness is different from the more frequent half-and-half kind of awareness in which intentions have become robotized. True, these mechanical or habit mechanisms can labor and thus free the purer consciousness for more important things. The trouble begins, however, when man doesn't use his residual consciousness but settles instead for mechanical intentions and implementations.

Wilson, *in toto,* refuses to settle for such mechanized behavior. He attacks the assumption that habits and appetites are natural and inevitable and, as such, beyond man's control. *Man can save himself* is the hopeful theme which permeates all of Wilson's work. This belief is the premise of the rationale which justifies his novels, it is woven into the biased patterns of his critical essays, and it is the mainspring of his philosophy. In developing his arguments, Wilson goes beyond the original metaphor of the robot, of course, for a robot is finally too limited an analogue for the complexities of mechanized consciousness. But the figure efficiently and boldly italicizes the *deadness* of that dominating and limited consciousness which has been accepted as the outer limit of awareness by behaviorists. When Wilson asks that man regain his control over the dead-weight of automated consciousness by using that all-important one percent, he seems to delight in the bad odds. Only a hero, veritably, bets on such a low probability; but *vive* the hero!

III New Pathways in Psychology

Wilson's goal as prophetic philosopher is more clearly defined than ever in his book-length exploration of the importance of certain recent psychological insights. Wilson's personal friendship with the American psychologist, the late Abraham Maslow, and his resulting introjection of many of Maslow's ideas over a period of years peaked in 1972 — as Wilson's enthusiasms always do — in another book. Optimistically entitled *New Pathways in Psychology*,[6] the work unavoidably contains some repetition of theories and supportive evidence presented by Wilson in earlier publications; but this volume, like the synoptic *Introduction to the New Existentialism*, is an open-ended summary of what Colin Wilson is all about. Students, critics, and others interested in Wilson are well advised to make use of its select bibliography, index, heuristic summaries, case studies, and suggestions for research along these new pathways.

After some personal comments about his relationship with Maslow and a review of definitions of key terms such as Maslow's "peak experience" and Wilson's "St. Neot's margin" (both explicated in this study), Wilson outlines his own modest qualification concerning Maslow's search for longer and better peak experiences. Wilson would move more quickly and more easily toward ways of increasing awareness intentionally. Perceiving the physical universe, which is the "objective world of things" (25), requires only sense receptors. Thus Wilson can reasonably assume that a cow, for example, which inhabits the objective world, ordinarily copes with its basic problems without much of a mind. Man, like the cow, must also cope with the basic level, the "first world"; but, because he has a mind, he is also confronted with a second world which is subjective. All humans are familiar with these two basic worlds, for both are functions of ordinary sensations and humdrum perceptions built out of those sensations. They help one survive physically.

Maslow and Wilson, however, do not stop there. Equating Sir Karl Popper's "third world, the world of objective contents of thought," with Teilhard de Chardin's "noosphere," or the world of the mind, Wilson exhorts men to confront this extrapolated *third* world as a *real* place: " . . . it is there all the time, like China or the moon; and it ought to be possible for me to go there at any time, leaving behind the boring person who is called by my name. It is fundamentally a world of pure *meaning*" (26).

The difference between the italicized *real* and the italicized *meaning* of the third world and the ordinary "real" and "meaning" of the second world results from the fact that the latter world is overwhelmed by "trivial, personal meaning, distorted and one-sided, a worm's eye view of meaning." Entrance into the third world requires both will and energy, for he who enters it has to be able to counteract the boredom of robotlike habits adopted as an easy adjustment to the two lower worlds. This third world invites, therefore, the strong and the brave to explore it. "It is man's evolutionary destiny to become a citizen of the third world," Wilson predicts, "to explore it as he might now explore Switzerland on a holiday" (26).

Few would resist the invitation to explore that brave new world envisioned by thinkers like Teilhard de Chardin, Karl Popper, Maslow, and Wilson; but the passports and the guide books are too often vague or hortatory rather than informative. To Wilson's credit, he tries to bring his readers down the abstraction ladder by specifying his terms and his goals through case studies and other citations rather than merely praising the benefits of awareness. Many prophets have exhorted men to hunt for transcendents, to open their minds and their hearts to higher meanings. Finding the *how* to the desirable goal of increased awareness, however, is for Wilson a disciplined procedure. He admits that religion, for example, could increase understanding in men, but he finds evidence that most religious practices do just the opposite, being too authoritarian. As things stand now, religion in general "fails to carry much conviction for the highly sophisticated and neurotic — who are the very ones who need it most" (40). Other means must be found, ones which do not require intellectual dishonesty or simplistic minds.

After Maslow's death, Wilson thought it imperative to explicate his friend's position, but he realized he must expand the book he had first intended to confine to the life and works of his friend. There were also cogent reasons for extending the topic to include the work of others, such as Erwin Straus, Medard Boss, William Glasser, Ronald Laing, and not least of all Wilson himself. Thus the finished work characteristically includes much more than Wilson had first intended. Even then it ends with a call to begin: "The discoveries I have tried to outline in this book are all so new that we have only just begun to explore their possibilities. Only one thing can be said with any certainty: the most interesting part is still to come" (270).

Wilson theorizes that man's higher needs and his aspirations toward increased awareness and peak experiences are "as instinctoid as the lower, as much a part of man's subconscious drives" (164). He believes that Maslow did not detail this revolutionary idea clearly enough; consequently, Maslow's approach seems elitist. Wilson invites each man to begin to *intend* to have his own peak experiences, to will them into existence without outside aids such as drugs. "Think of 'intentions,'" he advises, "as being needles of light, exploring the world's pitted surface; when used with delicacy and accuracy, and the results are sufficiently amplified by close attention, the result is a revelation of meaning" (269). He illustrates his metaphor with a homely example. He advises one to look at a picture, preferably a colored photograph of a landscape, "to look at it slowly and carefully, thinking of the eyes as the projectors of needlelike intentions. An ordinary glance at the picture seems to reveal most of its meaning; but after this first glance, treat the picture as a record of hidden meanings, waiting for the needle of light to search them out and re-create them in all their richness" (269).

Time is always of the essence. Wilson's significance to literature and philosophy inevitably will fluctuate until partisan opinions settle into objective evaluations. The real state of affairs is never distorted — only man's view of it is subject to distortion. One man's hero may appear to be another man's enemy without either the admirer or the detractor being in bad faith. Youthful seekers after the truth about themselves and about their world overlook more easily a prophet's awkward "style" than do their elders, for whom elegance can be more satisfying than vitality. The fact that Wilson was not a university graduate has been more important in England than in the United States. Certainly much of the hostility in England which helped distort the facts about his work was a snobbish rejection of Wilson's urgency, which seemed crude if not rude to critics writing leisurely reviews for established periodicals.

Americans, especially American youths, have not been unduly influenced by Wilson's humble origins. They have neither glorified him nor rejected him out-of-hand because he is self-taught. Colin Wilson will finally be tried, however, in many courts — by his peers, by his inferiors, and by his putative superiors, and in all fairness he has nothing to fear. He has begun clearly to validate his own work. As a new existentialist he is his own best witness that he is a good man.

Notes and References

Chapter One

1. Sidney R. Campion, *The World of Colin Wilson: A Biographical Study* (London, 1962), p. xiv. In the foreword to the study, which Campion had first shown him in 1959, Wilson explains that he had asked Campion to concentrate on his ideas rather than on his life. Eventually Wilson and Campion compromised on the present work, which is enthusiastically pro-Wilson.

2. *Voyage to a Beginning: An Intellectual Autobiography* (New York, 1969), p. 1. Page references to this work are given in the text in parentheses after each citation.

3. Campion, *The World of Colin Wilson,* pp. 211 - 12.

4. Both terms refer to meta-experiences which today interest parapsychologists. William James experienced panicky consciousness-expansions which he called "vastations." The contemporary psychologist, Abraham Maslow, emphasizes "peak experiences" as indices to the kind of intensity human awareness might attain. See chapters 3 and 7 below.

5. Campion, *The World of Colin Wilson,* p. 59.

6. Colin Wilson's canon is complicated by the fact that he sometimes announces works before they have been published. Impatient with practical details, he counts his productions in terms of plans as well as performances. The trait may be endearing to all but bibliographers.

7. Hopkins's one novel, *The Divine and the Decay* (London, 1957), was stillborn. The opening sentence echoes the keynote of outsiderism: "All the way out from England he was conscious of his loneliness." The hero, Plowart by name, says of himself: "An instinct warned me to shun people before I was contaminated" (7).

Stuart Holroyd was the youngest member of the trio who were identified as the religious wing of the Angry Young Men. Like Wilson, he was first published by Gollancz. Holroyd's essay, *Emergence from Chaos* (London, 1957), is calmer than Wilson's first book. As for the "influences problem," one may fairly assume that Holroyd and Wilson influenced each other about equally. Of course, they also had common sources of inspiration. In 1959, young Holroyd published his autobiography, *Flight and Pursuit* (London, 1959), an earnest statement of faith in "that evolutionary advance which would alone make all the tragedy and all the suffering meaningful" (237).

8. Angus Wilson had recommended his own publisher, Secker and Warburg, to Colin. When young Wilson showed his manuscript to Fred Warburg, the publisher seemed bored; but he phoned the young man twenty-four hours later "in great excitement" and offered him a contract. Wilson refused Warburg's offer, however, because the publisher wanted several alterations. Colin Wilson knew nothing about rejections in those days.

9. Anon., "Intellectual Thriller," review of *The Outsider, Time* LXVIII (July 2, 1956), 80.

10. See Campion, *The World of Colin Wilson,* pp. 13 ff.

11. The popular magazines exploited Wilson's youth and the sleeping-bag episodes but generally regarded him as another English "egg-head."

12. Kenneth Allsop, *The Angry Decade* (London, 1958), p. 162. Allsop also refers to "the ingenuous honesty with which he [Wilson] blows the gaff on the processes of writing" in the autobiographical introduction to *Religion and the Rebel,* the second volume in the Outsider cycle, wherein Wilson explains how he "came to 'dash off' *The Outsider*" (161).

13. Campion, *The World of Colin Wilson,* p. 132.

14. Perry Miller, Review of *Religion and the Rebel, New York Herald Tribune Book Review* (November 24, 1957), p. 10.

15. See, for example, *Newsweek* (Dec. 17, 1956), p. 54, in which Wilson was accused of admitting he was a fraud.

16. Wilson has always been determined to succeed also as a dramatist. This particular rejection saddened him for he believed that the Royal Court had promised him a chance. The play, Wilson reports in *Voyage,* was rejected with a printed slip only (238).

17. Anon., "About a Hobby — Murder," *Newsweek* (March 14, 1960), p. 105.

18. Allsop, *The Angry Decade,* p. 23.

Chapter Two

1. All references are to the American edition: *The Outsider* (Boston, 1956). Page references to this work (and to all other works by Colin Wilson as they are subsequently examined) are given in the text in parentheses after each citation.

2. *The Outsider* is not indexed, but there are almost two hundred separate name-entries alone in my informal card catalog. Anyone attempting to check all Wilson's sources (as I once tried) marvels at his thirst for knowledge.

3. Wilson's original title for *The Outsider* was *The Pain Threshold.* Later

Wilson refines his definition of the pain threshold, calling it the "St. Neot's margin," q.v. below.

4. Wilson has reported that he has received many fan letters from young readers. Every American campus has a group of enthusiastic supporters of Colin Wilson's ideas, youths who look upon him as a prophet.

5. Kingsley Amis, "The Legion of the Lost," *Spectator* CXCVI (June 15, 1956), 830.

6. Anon., Review of *The Outsider, Times Literary Supplement* (June 8, 1956), p. 1550.

7. All references are to the American edition: *Religion and the Rebel* (Boston, 1957).

8. Wilson criticizes Toynbee's method without seeming to recognize it as similar to his own. Writing of Toynbee's approach to his subject, he says: "At the first glance, it would seem to be romantic and 'literary.' Almost every page has some quotation from the Bible, or Greek drama, or poetry, or the Church Fathers, and it would hardly be untrue to say that, wherever he can, he prefers to express a thought in somebody else's words rather than his own" (121).

9. *Bernard Shaw: A Reassessment* (New York, 1969).

10. Perry Miller, Review of *Religion and the Rebel, New York Herald Tribune Book Review* (Nov. 24, 1957), p. 10.

11. Robert Peel, Review of *Religion and the Rebel, Christian Science Monitor* (Nov. 14, 1957), p. 7.

12. All references here are to the American edition: *The Stature of Man* (Boston, 1959).

13. Edmund Fuller, Review of *The Stature of Man, Saturday Review* XLII (Dec. 19, 1959), 35.

14. Irving Howe, Review of *The Stature of Man, New York Times Book Review* (Nov. 15, 1959), p. 6.

15. Robert Peel, Review of *The Stature of Man, Christian Science Monitor* (Dec. 24, 1959), p. 7.

16. Anon., Review of *The Stature of Man, Times Literary Supplement* (Sept. 4, 1959),p. 503.

Chapter Three

1. All references are to the American edition: *The Strength to Dream* (Boston, 1962).

2. Cf. Thomas S. Szasz, *Ideology and Insanity* (New York, 1970).

3. Benjamin DeMott, "Musclemen and Dreamers," *Harper's Magazine* CCXXV (October, 1962), 90.

4. Anon., Review of *The Strength to Dream, Encounter* XIX (August, 1962), 80.

5. Francis Hope, "All Those Fish," *Spectator* CCVIII (April 27, 1962), 558.

6. All references here are to the American edition: *Origins of the Sexual Impulse* (New York, 1963).

7. Maurice Richardson, Review of *Origins of the Sexual Impulse, New Statesman* LXV (May 24, 1963), 798.

8. Robert Maurer, Review of *Origins, New York Herald Tribune Books* (June 23, 1963), p. 10.

9. Eric Moon, Review of *Origins, Library Journal* LXXXVIII (May 1, 1963), 1892.

10. All references are to the American edition: *Beyond the Outsider* (Boston, 1965). In a prefatory comment, Wilson evinces surprise that no one had noticed that he was producing a "cycle."

11. Wilson also refers to this concept as the "Saint Neot's Margin." In an essay written for a symposium on humanistic psychology, Wilson tells how once, when he was hitchhiking, he felt depressed and bored. After finally getting a ride from a lorry driver, he experienced no elation; and, when the ride was abruptly terminated because of engine failure, he was not annoyed. He merely felt flat. But during his next lift, near the town of St. Neot in Huntingdonshire, after the threat of a similar kind of engine failure disappeared, Wilson felt elated. Introspecting about his unexpected change of mood, he concluded that the important element in the experience was the sudden awareness of freedom stimulated by the threat of inconvenience in the *second* engine failure. Thus he found an area of the human psyche that can be stimulated by pain or inconvenience but not by pleasure. Boredom and apathy, he is convinced, are functions of the absence of "involvement, commitment, participation." "Existential Psychology: A Novelist's Approach" in J. F. T. Bugental (editor), *Challenges of Humanistic Psychology* (New York, 1967), pp. 69 - 78.

12. Wilson here changes the initial letter of "Outsider" to lower case. This study, however, has kept the proper noun.

13. Marshall Cohen, "Beyond Belief," *New Statesman* LXIX (Jan. 15, 1965), 80.

14. Antony Flew, "Outsiders Two," *Spectator* CCXIV (Jan. 29, 1965), 140.

15. Añon., Review of *Beyond the Outsider, Christian Century* LXXXII (March 24, 1965), 369.

16. Anon., Review of *Beyond the Outsider, Times Literary Supplement* (Jan. 28, 1965), p. 71.

Chapter Four

1. *Declaration* (London, 1958), p. 58.
2. Colin Wilson in a recent letter to the author of this study.

3. All references are to the first American edition: *Ritual in the Dark* (Boston, 1960). Wilson had called one of the early drafts *Things Do Not Happen*, a title indicating his refusal to settle for the *given* universe.

4. See Wayne C. Booth, *The Rhetoric of Fiction* (Chicago, 1961). Booth has analyzed the various dimensions of "distance" and degrees of "reliability." Wilson would qualify as a sophisticated novelist employing ambiguity and irony to achieve higher levels of truth; but the conservative Booth, of course, does not mention Colin Wilson.

5. The cases of Landru and Peace are both analyzed in *Encyclopaedia of Murder*.

6. Phoebe Adams, Review of *Ritual in the Dark, Atlantic Monthly* CCV (March, 1960), 114.

7. Walter Allen, Review of *Ritual, New York Times Book Review* (March 6, 1960), p. 4.

8. Gene Baro, Review of *Ritual, New York Herald Tribune Book Review* (March 6, 1960), p. 5.

9. Anon., Review of *Ritual, Time* LXXV (March 7, 1960), 102.

10. Anon., Review of *Ritual, Twentieth Century* (London) LXIX (June, 1960), 579.

11. All references are to the American edition: *Adrift in Soho* (Boston, 1961). Sidney Campion in *The World of Colin Wilson* quotes a letter from Wilson acknowledging his "use" of anecdotes from a manuscript by a Charles Russell — who resembles the Charles Compton Street of Wilson's novel (233 - 35).

12. R. H. W. Dillard, "Toward an Existential Realism: the Novels of Colin Wilson," *The Hollins Critic* IV (October, 1967), 8.

13. Robert O. Bowen, Review of *Adrift in Soho, National Review* XIII (Dec. 2, 1961), 384.

14. Martin Levin, Review of *Adrift, New York Times Book Review* (Oct. 15, 1961), p. 48.

15. John Fuller, Review of *Adrift, The Listener* LXXVI (Sept. 7, 1961), 361.

16. Paul Pickrel, "Scum and Dregs," *Harper's Magazine* CCXXIII (November, 1961), 110.

17. All references are to the American edition: *The Violent World of Hugh Greene* (Boston, 1963). The novel was published in England as *The World of Violence* (London, 1963).

18. D. A. N. Jones, Review of *Violent World, New Statesman* LXV (June 14, 1963), 910.

19. All references are to the American paperback edition: *The Sex Diary of Gerard Sorme* (New York, 1964). The work was published in England as *Man Without a Shadow: The Diary of an Existentialist* (London, 1963).

20. See Preface to the English edition.

21. Stanley Kauffmann, Review of *Sex Diary, New Republic* CXLVIII (May, 1962), 32.

22. R. G. G. Price, Review of *Sex Diary, Punch* CCXLV (Nov. 6, 1963), 683.
23. *The Mind Parasites*, p. xx.

Chapter Five

1. All references are to the American edition: *Necessary Doubt* (New York, 1964). An introductory note warns that no personal resemblance between Zweig and Tillich was intended.
2. Anon., Review of *Necessary Doubt, Times Literary Supplement* (Feb. 27, 1964), p. 161.
3. Lester Goran, Review of *Necessary Doubt, Chicago Sunday Tribune Books Today* (August 30, 1964), p. 6.
4. John Fuller, Review of *Necessary Doubt, New Statesman*, LXVII (March 20, 1964), 460.
5. M. M., Review of *Necessary Doubt, Christian Science Monitor* (Sept. 24, 1964), p. 7.
6. All references are to the American edition: *The Glass Cage* (New York, 1966).
7. M. K. Grant, Review of *The Glass Cage, Library Journal*, XCII (June, 1967), 2180.
8. See the lurid picture of a "fiendish sadist" making love to a beautiful woman on the cover of the English paperback edition: Pan Books, London, 1968.
9. Anon., Review of *The Glass Cage, Times Literary Supplement* (Nov. 3, 1966), p. 1008.
10. All references are to the American edition: *The Mind Parasites* (Sauk City, 1967). The quotation is from *Preface*, p. xx.
11. H. P. Lovecraft, *Dagon and Other Macabre Tales* (Sauk City, 1965).
12. *Ibid.*, p. 412.
13. All references are to the English edition: *The Philosopher's Stone* (London, 1969).
14. See R. H. W. Dillard, *op. cit.*, p. 12.
15. See, for example, Herbert A. Otto, "New Light on the Human Potential," *Saturday Review*, LII (Dec. 20, 1969), 14-17.
16. Anon., "Shazam!" Review of *The Philosopher's Stone, Times Literary Supplement* (July 10, 1969), p. 745.
17. Barry Cole, "Traveller's Tales," *Spectator* XXII (June 28, 1969), 857.
18. James Fenton, "Fossil Remains," *New Statesman* LXXVII (June 27, 1966), 916.
19. All references are to the American edition: *Lingard* (New York, 1970). The novel was published in England as *The Killer*, 1970.
20. Henry Tube, "Thrills and Spills," *Spectator* CCXXIV (May 30, 1970), 718.

21. Derek Mahon, "Games and Cases," *The Listener* LXXXIII (May 21, 1970), 693.
22. All references are to the English edition: *The God of the Labyrinth* (London, 1970). The novel was also published in paperback as *The Hedonists* (New York, 1971).
23. Anon., Review of *The God of the Labyrinth, Times Literary Supplement* (June 18, 1970), p. 653.
24. Clive Jordan, "Dogbitten," *New Statesman* LXXIX (June 26, 1970), 920.
25. Maurice Capitanchik, Review of *The God of the Labyrinth, Spectator* CCXXIV (June 27, 1970), 852.
26. All references are to *The Black Room* (London, 1971).
27. All references are to *The Schoolgirl Murder Case* (London, 1974).

Chapter Six

1. All references are to *Eagle and Earwick* (London, 1965). The quotation is from page 30.
2. All references are to the American edition: *Chords and Discords* (New York, 1966). This edition contains a chapter on American music not included in the first English edition, which was entitled *Brandy of the Damned* (1964).
3. "Manufacturing a tradition" is, of course, a contradiction in terms; but Wilson, like Humpty Dumpty, often makes words mean what he wants them to mean.
4. J. Raymond, Review of *Chords and Discords, Punch* CCLII (Feb. 8, 1967), 209.
5. P. L. Miller, Review of *Chords and Discords, Library Journal* XCI (Oct. 1, 1966), 4667.
6. Jeremy Noble, Review of *Chords and Discords, New Statesman* LXVIII (Dec. 11, 1964), 923.
7. Cf. the novels *Lingard, Ritual in the Dark, The Glass Cage,* and *The Schoolgirl Murder Case.*
8. All references are to the English edition: *Encyclopaedia of Murder* (London, 1961).
9. Esther Howard, Review of *Encyclopaedia, Spectator* CCVII (Dec. 22, 1961), 934.
10. All references are to *A Casebook of Murder* (London, 1969).
11. Phoebe Adams, Review of *A Casebook, Atlantic Monthly* CCXXV (May, 1967), 132.
12. References are to *Order of Assassins* (London, 1972).
13. Anon., Review of *Order of Assassins, Times Literary Supplement* (Dec. 8, 1972), p.1507.

14. All references are to the American edition: *Rasputin and the Fall of the Romanovs* (New York, 1964).
15. Oleg Ivsky, Review of *Rasputin, Library Journal* CXXXIX (October 15, 1964), 3952.
16. Robert Payne, Review of *Rasputin, New York Times Book Review* (Dec. 13, 1964), p. 20.
17. All references are to the American edition: *Bernard Shaw: A Reassessment* (New York, 1969).
18. Keith Cushman, Review of *Bernard Shaw, Library Journal* XCIV (Oct. 1, 1969), 3452.
19. Stanley Weintraub, Review of *Bernard Shaw, New York Times Book Review* (Nov. 9, 1969), p. 18.
20. D. J. Leary, Review of *Bernard Shaw, Saturday Review* LII (Nov. 15, 1969), 53.
21. Both versions are referred to in the text.
22. Anon., Review of *Poetry and Mysticism, Times Literary Supplement* (Feb. 5, 1971), p. 153.
23. All references are to the American edition: *The Occult* (New York, 1971).
24. Anon., Review of *The Occult, Choice* IX (April, 1972), 200.
25. Anon., Review of *The Occult, Times Literary Supplement* (Nov. 26, 1971), p. 1471.
26. Joyce Carol Oates, Review of *The Occult, The American Poetry Journal* II (January/February, 1973), 8 - 9.
27. All references are to *Sex and the Intelligent Teenager* (London, 1966).

Chapter Seven

1. *See Pierre Thevanaz, What Is Phenomenology?* (Chicago, 1962).
2. *Ibid.*, p. 5.
3. All references are to the American edition: *Introduction to the New Existentialism* (Boston, 1967).
4. James F. T. Bugental, ed., *Challenges of Humanistic Psychology* (New York, 1967).
5. *Ibid.*, p. 73.
6. All references are to the American edition: *New Pathways in Psychology: Maslow and the Post-Freudian Revolution* (New York, 1972).

Selected Bibliography

PRIMARY SOURCES

This bibliography of Colin Wilson's writing includes in chronological order all book-length works (American and British hardcover and paperback) to date (1974) but only several of Wilson's numerous shorter pieces, because the contents of Wilson's "articles" are usually subsumed in later books. Also, none of the proliferating translations are listed. In general, the bibliography is adjusted to the convenience of the American reader and to the availability of texts in this country although the British edition of each work is listed first whenever it was published first. See also the bibliography in R. H. W. Dillard, *op. cit.*, for Canadian editions, and Sidney Campion, *op. cit.*, for otherwise unpublished extracts from letters and journals.

The Outsider. London: Victor Gollancz, 1956; Boston: Houghton Mifflin, 1956; London: Pan Books (paper), 1967; New York: Delta (paper), 1967.

Religion and the Rebel. London: Victor Gollancz, 1957; Boston: Houghton Mifflin, 1957.

"Beyond the Outsider." *Declaration*, Ed. Tom Maschler; London: MacGibbon & Kee, 1958; New York: Dutton, 1958.

The Age of Defeat. London: Victor Gollancz, 1959. As *The Stature of Man*. Boston: Houghton Mifflin, 1959.

Ritual in the Dark. London: Victor Gollancz, 1960; Boston: Houghton Mifflin, 1960; New York: Popular Library (paper), 1961; London: Pan Books (paper), 1962.

Encyclopaedia of Murder (with Pat Pitman). London: Arthur Barker, 1961; New York: G. P. Putman's Sons, 1962; London: Pan Books (paper), 1964.

Adrift in Soho. London: Victor Gollancz, 1961; Boston: Houghton Mifflin, 1961; London: Pan Books (paper), 1964.

The Strength to Dream: Literature and the Imagination. London: Victor Gollancz, 1962; Boston: Houghton Mifflin, 1962.

The World of Violence. London: Victor Gollancz, 1963; London: Pan Books (paper), 1965. As *The Violent World of Hugh Greene*. Boston: Houghton Mifflin, 1963.

Origins of the Sexual Impulse. London: Arthur Barker, 1963; New York: G. P. Putnam's Sons, 1963; London: Panther Books (paper), 1966.

Man Without a Shadow: The Diary of an Existentialist. London: Arthur Barker, 1963; London: Pan Books (paper), 1966. As *The Sex Diary of Gerard Sorme*. New York: The Dial Press, 1963. New York: Pocket Books (paper), 1964.

Necessary Doubt. London: Arthur Barker, 1964; New York: Simon and Schuster, 1964; London: Panther Books (paper), 1966; New York: Pocket Books (paper), 1966.

Rasputin and the Fall of the Romanovs. London: Arthur Barker, 1964; New York: Farrar, Straus and Co., 1964; London: Panther Books (paper), 1966.

Brandy of the Damned: Discoveries of a Musical Eclectic. London: John Baker, 1964; Revised editions as *Chords and Discords: Purely Personal Opinions on Music*. New York: Crown, 1966; and *Colin Wilson on Music*. London: Pan Books (paper), 1967.

Beyond the Outsider: The Philosophy of the Future. London: Arthur Barker, 1965; Boston: Houghton Mifflin, 1965; London: Pan Books (paper), 1965.

Eagle and Earwig. London: John Baker, 1965.

Sex and the Intelligent Teenager. London: Arrow Books (paper), 1966.

The Glass Cage: An Unconventional Detective Story. London: Arthur Barker, 1966; New York: Random House, 1967; London: Pan Books (paper), 1968

Introduction to the New Existentialism. London: Hutchinson, 1966; Boston: Houghton Mifflin, 1967; Boston: Houghton Mifflin (paper), 1967.

The Mind Parasites. London: Arthur Barker, 1967; Sauk City, Wisconsin: Arkham House, 1967; London: Pan Books (paper), 1969.

"Existential Psychology: A Novelist's Approach." *Challenges of Humanistic Psychology*. Ed. James F. T. Bugental. New York: McGraw-Hill, 1967.

The Philosopher's Stone. London: Arthur Barker, 1969; New York: Crown, 1971. New York: Warner Paperback Library, 1971.

Voyage to a Beginning: An Intellectual Autobiography. London: Cecil and Amelia Woolf, 1969; New York: Crown, 1969.

Bernard Shaw: A Reassessment. London: Hutchinson, 1969; New York: Atheneum, 1969.

A Casebook of Murder. London: Leslie Frewin, 1969; London: Mayflower (paper), 1971.

Poetry and Mysticism. San Francisco: City Lights Press, 1969; London: Hutchinson, 1970 (expanded version).

The God of the Labyrinth. London: Rupert Hart-Davis, 1970; London: Mayflower (paper), 1971. As *The Hedonists*. New York: New American Library, 1971.

The Killer. London: New English Library, 1970. As *Lingard*. New York: Crown Publishers, 1970.

The Strange Genius of David Lindsay. With J. B. Pick and E. H. Visiak. London: John Baker, 1970.
Strindberg: Playscript 31. London: Calder and Boyars, 1970.
The Black Room. London: Weidenfeld and Nicolson, 1971.
The Occult. New York: Random House, 1971. London: Hodder and Stoughton, 1971.
New Pathways in Psychology: Maslow and the Post-Freudian Revolution. New York: Taplinger Publishing Company, 1972. London: Victor Gollancz, 1972.
Order of Assassins. London: Rupert Hart-Davis, 1972.
The Schoolgirl Murder Case. London: Hart-Davis, MacGibbon,1974. New York: Crown, 1974.

SECONDARY SOURCES

1. *Selected Criticism of Colin Wilson's Writings*

This list includes all significant book-length studies but only a sampling from the hundreds of review articles consulted in the preparation of this study.

ANON. Review of *The Outsider. Times Literary Supplement,* June 8, 1956, p. 342. Typically friendly review of the kind that prepared the way for later reversals of opinion: "The charm of this book arises from its faults."
———. Review of *Chords and Discords. Times Literary Supplement,* Dec. 3, 1964, p. 1100. Typical quasi-contradictory qualification: ". . . shrewd observations . . . based on a faulty aesthetic . . . often well founded in psychology."
———. Review of *Beyond the Outsider. Times Literary Supplement,* Jan. 28, 1965, p. 71. The evaluation, although characteristically qualified, ends in praise: ". . . an argument which, if it is not quite adequately sustained, is yet . . . both tenable and heartening."
———. Review of *Voyage to a Beginning. Times Literary Supplement,* Nov. 11, 1969, p. 1275. Praises Wilson's courage as an autodidact and pioneer: "We must treat Mr. Wilson with respect. Where we disagree with him as an author we must admire him as a man."
ALLSOP, KENNETH. *The Angry Decade.* London: Peter Owen, 1958. Responsible "survey of the cultural revolt of the 1950's." Includes a chapter ("The Law-givers") on the Colin Wilson phenomenon of 1956 from the perspective of a close, not unsympathetic observer.
AMIS, KINGSLEY. "The Legion of the Lost," *Spectator* CXCVI (June 15, 1956), 830. Amis's review of *The Outsider* strikes an antiintellectual note distasteful to the "Establishment." Amis admits that he has never heard of Barbusse, Sartre, Camus, Kierkegaard, Nietzsche, Hesse, Hemingway, Van Gogh, Nijinsky, Tolstoy, Dostoevski, George

Fox, Blake, Ramakrishna, Gurdjieff, Hulme "and a large number of bit players" in *The Outsider*.

BLANC, ROBERT J. "Captain Ahab, The Outsider," *English Record* XVIII (Oct., 1967), 10 - 14. Wilson's Outsider-syndrome applied to a literary character. Ahab shares the characteristics Wilson ascribes to his Outsider: "endurance of loneliness, desire for spiritual freedom, aversion to organized religion, and faith in spirit to overcome matter."

CAMPION, SIDNEY R. *The World of Colin Wilson*. London: Frederick Muller, 1962. The first (and only until this present study) book-length essay on Colin Wilson; valuable for excerpts from diaries and letters not printed elsewhere as well as commendable for pioneering support of the young philosopher-writer whom Campion clearly admires.

DE MOTT, BENJAMIN. Review of *Strength to Dream. Harper's Magazine* CCXXV (Oct., 1962), 90. Qualified indictment of Wilson as a "Nietzschean hipster."

DILLARD, R. H. W. "Toward an Existential Realism: The Novels of Colin Wilson." *The Hollins Critic* IV (Oct., 1967). Astute and friendly analysis of Wilson's fiction through *The Mind Parasites*. Praises Wilson as "a young man of real vision" (12). Contains a bibliography through 1967, including Canadian editions.

FORD, BORIS, ed. *The Modern Age: The Pelican Guide to English Literature*, VII. Baltimore: Penguin Books, 1961. Collection of critical essays on modern British literature typical of the "Establishment." Wilson is dismissed in two brief references.

FULLER, JOHN. Review of *Necessary Doubt. New Statesman* LXVII (Mar. 20, 1964), 460. Flippant review of Wilson's solemn novel: "Dr. Fell met Dr. Zweig."

GORAN, LESTER. Review of *Necessary Doubt. Chicago Sunday Tribune Books Today*, Aug. 30, 1964, p. 6. Reviewer calls the structure of the novel "creaky" and the characters "absurd," but adds also that "Wilson has a narrative energy that makes the reader forgive him."

HOWE, IRVING. Review of *The Stature of Man. New York Times Book Review*, Nov. 15, 1959, p. 6. Critical attack typical of the backlash; denounces the third volume in the Outsider cycle as "a smorgasbord for the half-educated."

KAUFFMANN, STANLEY. Review of *Sex Diary of Gerard Sorme. New Republic* CXLVIII (May, 1963), 32. Suggests Wilson is a "spoof" created by Amis, Muggeridge, and Ustinov.

KRUTCH, JOSEPH WOOD. Review of *The Outsider. Saturday Review*, XXXIX (Sept. 8, 1956), 37. Despite serious qualifications, predicts that the term "Outsider" will become as useful as Sinclair Lewis's "Babbitt."

MILLER, PERRY. Review of *Religion and the Rebel. New York Herald Tribune Book Review*, Nov. 24, 1957, p. 10. "To call these essays sophomoric is to dignify them," the reviewer begins; then he concedes that Wilson may be a "portent."

OATES, JOYCE CAROL. "Introduction to *The Philosopher's Stone.*" *The Philosopher's Stone,* New York: Warner Paperback Library, 1974, pp. 7 - 15. Groups Wilson with John Fowles, Doris Lessing, and Margaret Drabble as "especially exciting because they are struggling to express . . . our crucial contemporary problem . . ." (7).

———. Review of *The Occult. The American Poetry Review* II (Jan./Feb., 1973), 8 - 9. Enthusiastic endorsement of Wilson's work: "I cannot recommend it too highly" (9).

PRIESTLEY, J. B. "Thoughts on the Outsider." *The New Statesman and Nation* LII (July 7, 1956), 10 - 11. Wilson's first book is called a "dashing study" which has had "a well-deserved success" — typical of the band-wagon praise which lasted only several months.

RICHARDSON, MAURICE. Review of *Origins of the Sexual Impulse. New Statesman* LXV (May 24, 1963), 789. Witty and hostile: ". . . a kind of poor man's Krafft-Ebbing. . . . It is staggering how anyone who has read so much can get so many things wrong."

TODD, OLIVER. "Colin Wilson Ou Le *Lumpen*-Intellectuel." *Temps Modernes* (Paris) CLII (Aug. 14, 1958), 748-54. A review of French translation of *The Outsider (L'homme en dehors);* resolves controversy over the work into a matter of taste.

WALSH, CHAD. Review of *The Stature of Man. Chicago Sunday Tribune,* Dec. 13, 1959, p. 2. Qualifies denunciation of the work as sophomoric with a *yet* clause insisting that it is important: typical self-contradictory response to middle volumes in Outsider cycle.

2. *Selected Background and Reference Works*

The needs of students rather than of sophisticated scholars were considered in compiling this list, and no attempt has been made to include the extensive library of items consulted in the preparation of this study.

BARRETT, WILLIAM. *What is Existentialism?* New York: Grove Press, 1964. Attempt to explicate the evolution of existentialism from Hegel to Heidegger. More sophisticated than Colin Wilson's analyses but equally fervent.

BECKER, HOWARD S. *Outsiders: Studies in the Sociology of Deviance.* New York: The Free Press, 1963. Not mentioned by Wilson, but an interesting correlative use of the term "Outsider" in a strictly sociological context. Becker's "Outsiders," unlike Wilson's, would yield to psychotherapy.

BOOTH, WAYNE C. *The Rhetoric of Fiction.* Chicago: University of Chicago Press, 1961. Solemn analysis of the "novelist's art," often pertinent to Wilson's fictions.

BUGENTAL, JAMES F. T., ed. *Challenges of Humanistic Psychology.* New York: McGraw-Hill, 1967. Important essays relevant to the kind of psychology which underpins Wilson's new existentialism. Includes an essay by Wilson. (See Primary Sources above.)

FARBER, MARVIN. *The Aims of Phenomenology.* New York: Harper Torchbooks, 1966. Critical introduction to phenomenology, with the emphasis on "motives, methods, and impact of Husserl's thought."

GUTMAN, JAMES, ed. *Philosophy A to Z.* New York: Grosset and Dunlap, 1963. Handy reference work based on the writings of Continental philosophers. Carefully edited; stylistically consistent.

HOLROYD, STUART. *Emergence from Chaos.* Boston: Houghton Mifflin, 1957. Correlative essay by Wilson's fellow member of the religious wing of the Angry Young Men.

———. *Flight and Pursuit: A Venture into Autobiography.* London: Victor Gollancz, 1959. Wilson's friend defends himself against the ill-natured attacks which followed *his* Outsider-type book. Includes an account of Holroyd's friendship with Colin Wilson and an appeal to the "few" to accomplish the much-needed "evolutionary advance."

JAMES, WILLIAM. *The Varieties of Religious Experience.* New York: Mentor Books, 1958. Reprint of the work by the famous American psychologist which much impressed Colin Wilson and which still defines a transcendent "philosophical temper."

KAUFMANN, WALTER, ed. *Existentialism from Dostoevsky to Satre.* New York: Meridian Books, 1957. Popular collection of pertinent excerpts from Kierkegaard, Nietzsche, Rilke, Kafka, Jaspers, and Camus in addition to the writers named in the title. Contains a readable introduction by Professor Kaufmann, whose values are made explicit.

KOCKELMANS, JOSEPH. *The Philosophy of Edmund Husserl and Its Interpretation.* Garden City: Doubleday (Anchor Book), 1967. Collection of explications and essays including extracts from the writings of leading phenomenologists and existentialists such as Husserl, Heidegger, Sartre, Merleau-Ponty, and others. Recommended for the student with neither time nor sophistication sufficient to investigate primary sources via the works of these important thinkers — not all of whom have yet been translated.

LOVECRAFT, H. P. *Dagon and Other Macabre Tales.* Sauk City, Wisconsin: Arkham House, 1965. Contains an introduction by Wilson's friend, August Derleth, and a 1926 essay by Lovecraft, "Supernatural Horror in Literature," which justifies such fantasies as Wilson's *The Mind Parasites.*

MASCHLER, TOM, ed. *Declaration.* London: MacGibbon & Kee, 1958. Collection of essays by members of the group (minus Kingsley Amis) who were identified as "angries" but who never really coalesced: Lindsay Anderson, Kenneth Tynan, Stuart Holroyd, John Osborne, Doris Lessing, Colin Wilson, Bill Hopkins, and John Wain. Wilson's essay, "Beyond the Outsider," contains nothing essential not found in his later books.

MASLOW, ABRAHAM. *Toward a Psychology of Being.* Princeton: D. Van Nostrand, 1962. Readable example of the kind of existential psychological theory which has been a major component in Wilson's new existentialism.

MAY, ROLLO, ed. *Existential Psychology.* New York: Random House, 1961. Relevant collection of essays by May, Maslow, Feifel, Rogers, Allport, and Lyons — from a 1959 "Symposium on Existential Psychology." Valuable as examples of the kinds of antibehaviorism that have reinforced Wilson's philosophical position.

PAUL, LESLIE. *Angry Young Men.* London: Faber & Faber, 1951. Pre-Outsider sets the tone as well as suggests a name for the rebels: "A tent, or even a sleeping-bag in the open air, was the longed for goal. . . ."

SARTRE, JEAN PAUL. *Being and Nothingness.* Trans. Hazel E. Barnes. New York: Philosophical Library, 1956. A major opus; difficult but essential to an understanding of the *old* existentialism.

SKINNER, B. F. *Science and Human Behavior.* New York: Macmillan, 1953. Bible of American behaviorism; generally anathema to the new existentialism.

———. *Walden Two.* New York: Macmillan, 1948. Bold projection of the good life in terms of behavioral engineering.

SYPHER, WILLIE. *Loss of the Self in Modern Literature and Art.* New York: Vintage Books, 1962. Responsible analysis of the existential rebellion produced and promoted by "Outsiders."

THEVENAZ, PIERRE. *What Is Phenomenology?* Chicago: Quadrangle Books, 1962. Four essays by an eminent phenomenologist. Includes a bibliography of the major works of Husserl, Heidegger, Sartre, and Merleau-Ponty.

WANN, T. W., ed. *Behaviorism and Phenomenology: Contrasting Bases for Modern Psychology.* Chicago: University of Chicago Press (Phoenix Books), 1964. Contains essays by B. F. Skinner and Carl Rogers, among others. Readable examples of the wide range of contemporary concerns.

WHITEHEAD, ALFRED NORTH. *Science and the Modern World.* New York: New American Library, 1925. Series of lectures on the power of reason; typical of the thinking which helped Wilson move toward his new existentialism.

Index

(The works of Colin Wilson are listed under his name)